WORLD WAR II

and

CHESTER COUNTY PENNSYLVANIA

WORLD WAR II
and
CHESTER COUNTY PENNSYLVANIA

Marion M. Piccolomini

The History Press

Published by The History Press
Charleston, SC
www.historypress.net

Front cover, clockwise left to right: Photo by Jimmy John. Chester County Historical Society, West Chester, PA; Used with permission of the Chalfant Collection; From the collections of the National Iron & Steel Heritage Museum, Coatesville, PA; Photo by Jimmy John. Chester County Historical Society, West Chester, PA. Back cover, top: Image courtesy of Longwood Gardens. Inset: Photo by Jimmy John. Chester County Historical Society, West Chester, PA.

First published 2016

Manufactured in the United States

ISBN 978.1.46711.846.0

Library of Congress Control Number: 2015956827

Contents

Preface

Before the Japanese attacked the U.S. Navy fleet at Pearl Harbor, Hawaii, on December 7, 1941, Chester County was a much different locale than it is today. Its population has quadrupled from 135,626 people living here in 1940 to more than 500,000 residents currently. Most of the small farms that dominated the landscape as late as 1960 now have morphed into suburbia, while many of the small towns are no longer economically sustained by locally owned manufacturing firms. Instead, many of those little urban burgs have evolved into bedroom communities, and most of their residents now commute daily to and from office parks, plants and distribution centers in surrounding parts of southeastern Pennsylvania and beyond.

As some 16 million American men and women left their jobs back home to serve in the military during the World War II years, that employment shift created a tremendous strain on the U.S. economy, which was booming with War Department orders for military supplies and equipment.

Meanwhile, many folks on the homefront, all across America, did their part by planting victory gardens, participating in scrap drives, becoming Red Cross volunteers, buying war bonds, participating in air raid drills and observing rationing rules that applied to gasoline, tires, certain food items and articles of clothing.

But since the war had such a huge impact on industrial firms in Chester County, which had been struggling to escape the confines of the Great Depression, it's appropriate that this preface initially focuses on the industrial aspect of the homefront. Following are examples of how several of Chester

County's major companies and their employees performed magnificently during the war.

One of the local industries that warrants significant attention in this book is Lukens Steel, once the county's largest employer. It's particularly noteworthy that one of Lukens's many accomplishments occurred before the U.S. officially entered the war when the Coatesville-based steel firm produced plates for several thousand "Liberty ships," which were used to transport military supplies and equipment from the United States to England. And most of the folks working at Lukens back then knew their efforts were appreciated because, for example, the April 3, 1944 edition of the company paper included a War Department telegram that described how a brigade of tanks, built with Lukens By-Products Division parts, had made an "amazing stand in Libya against two German panzer divisions." You'll also learn how many Lukens employees, encumbered by gasoline rationing like everyone else, applied a common-sense approach to reducing their cars' gas consumption while commuting back and forth to work.

Phoenix Iron Company had several unique challenges to overcome during the war period, especially resolution of conflicting policies promulgated by two federal wartime agencies. Despite those issues, the Phoenixville firm's employees set production records throughout those critical years.

Schramm Inc. in West Chester produced orders for the military during the World War II period. Some of those orders were for some unique equipment, such as small, portable "floodlight trailers." You'll also learn how Schramm employees took on a seemingly impossible task when they fulfilled a large order for generators, welders and compressor units in an incredibly short period of time. Completion of that project on schedule was the result of several innovative decisions. During the war, one innovative decision made by the company was to subcontract some of the production, warehousing and shipping responsibilities to local businesses that had not enjoyed a resurgence of business during the war years.

National Foam System Inc. was the first U.S. firm to manufacture a firefighting foam. One product—called Aer-O-Foam—was critical to the war effort because gasoline and oil fires were frequent byproducts of bombs and artillery. By 1943, National Foam's plant in West Chester was producing the foam around the clock. The foam also was used in all of the navy's firefighting schools, and it had been used to extinguish a fire on a tanker carrying aviation fuel that collided with a munitions ship off the shores of Norfolk, Virginia. As a result, the tanker and 75 percent of its cargo were saved.

Although the Downingtown Manufacturing Company had been producing huge paper-making equipment since the late nineteenth century, its contributions to the war effort were limited to smaller pieces of equipment. It was one of the thousands of companies across America that made a variety of equipment parts that were critical to the U.S. military. Two of those pieces of equipment were turret ring assemblies, which enabled tank guns to be turned easily and quickly, and breech mechanisms for weapons such as submarine deck guns.

But manufacturing by local industries was only one of Chester County's sectors that had an impact on the homefront during the World War II era. For example, many soldiers who were wounded in combat probably would have died of bacterial infections from their wounds if West Chester's G. Raymond Rettew had not figured out a way to mass-produce penicillin by applying techniques he had used in the mushroom business. After producing a "raw" concentrated form of penicillin solution in the Chester County Mushroom Laboratory in West Chester, he had the solution dehydrated by freeze-drying it. As a result of his efforts, large shipments of penicillin could be distributed to military medical outposts around the world.

One of the most unique volunteer services during the World War II era was the mailing of the *Coatesville Red Triangle* newsletter and sending fruitcakes at Christmastime to thousands of Chester County GIs. Both projects were a major undertaking by J. Irvie Hoffman, executive secretary of the Coatesville YMCA. The newsletters contained information about local sports teams, humor and excerpts of news retrieved from letters sent home by local service personnel. The cost of printing and mailing the newsletters and making and sending fruitcakes totaled about $250,000.

Local colleges were also impacted by the war. A long summer program was introduced at West Chester State Teachers College to speed up teacher training; and the college's students who ate at least twelve meals a week at an on-campus facility were required to turn in their food ration books. Since enrollment at the all-male Lincoln University, a historically black college in southern Chester County, had declined significantly because so many young men were in the military, excess dorm rooms were made available to people employed in defense jobs nearby. And students at Immaculata College in Malvern were required to take "defense" courses—such as first aid, home nursing, occupational therapy and nutrition—for one hour each week. Also, many young ladies attending Chester County Hospital's Nursing School participated in the U.S. Cadet Corps, an accelerated federal program that paid for their student nurses' training in exchange for a military service obligation.

The army's Valley Forge General Hospital, a ninety-eight-building complex, was opened near Phoenixville in 1943. The hospital had a major but indirect impact on that town and the surrounding area because it was staffed by hundreds of military medical professionals as well as civilian personnel who had to find rental units in the town since living quarters on the hospital post were limited. The local economy also got a boost from the thousands of friends and family who spent some time and money in Phoenixville while visiting patients at the hospital.

Obviously, this preface offers just a few snapshots of the many fascinating stories about Chester County's homefront. We hope you find as much enjoyment reading it as Marion Piccolomini did writing it.

Parry Desmond
Downingtown Area Historical Society

Acknowledgements

This book was inspired by the *Coatesville Red Triangle* newsletter, which was published during World War II by the YMCA. It was fascinating to read copies of the newsletters available at the Chester County Historical Society—not only were the soldier's letters captivating, it was inspiring to read about the community that made the effort to run the program. That original idea to write about the *Red Triangle* program grew into a journey through Chester County. There were so many contributions that the county made to the war effort, and at every destination there was someone or something that lead to the next story.

I would like to thank The History Press for not only considering my proposal but for suggesting that the book be expanded to include other homefront efforts in Chester County. I would also like to thank the editors I worked with at The History Press, Katie Stitely and Karmen Cook, who helped me work through this process.

There are so many people, businesses, organizations and institutions that provided resources and information for this project, from one fascinating story to another, that I would like to acknowledge. Their help and guidance to various sources of information were invaluable. The organizations that were generous of their time and resources include:

The American National Red Cross

The staff at the Chester County Historical Society—from photos to resources in the community, you were an unlimited resource. Thank you.

Downingtown Area Historical Society—thank you for the resources, special thanks to Parry for writing the preface and to Carol—it was through my work with you that my interest was sparked in the *Red Triangle* newsletter, and for that, I am grateful.

Hagley Museum and Library

Historical Society of the Phoenixville Area—thank you for access to your collection and for providing contacts in the community.

Longwood Gardens

National Iron & Steel Heritage Museum—thank you for access to your unlimited resources about Lukens Steel.

Special Collections Research Center, Temple University Libraries

Tredyffrin Easttown Historical Society—thank you for sharing resources about the war years.

University of Valley Forge—I appreciate the information about the Valley Forge General Hospital, especially the photo research.

West Nantmeal Township Historical Commission—thank you for sharing resources about the war years.

YMCA of Brandywine Valley—thank you, especially for the photograph and the story about the fruitcake box.

The institutions of higher education whose faculty and staff were generous of their time include: the Gabriele Library at Immaculata University, the Langston Hughes Memorial Library at Lincoln University and the Francis Harvey Green Library at West Chester University. Even though you were in the midst of preparation for the new semester, all of you fit me into your busy schedules. Thank you.

The businesses that were generous in their time and resources include:

National Foam Inc.—I appreciate the time and effort all of you took to research company records about the war years.

Schramm Inc.—to Mr. Schramm, thank you for taking the time to share information about the company's part in the mobilization effort.

There were also individuals who agreed to meet with me to talk about their experiences in the county during the war. The information all of you shared brought to life the spirit of Chester County during World War II. Thank you so much for allowing the readers to share your experiences: Margaret B. Chalfant, Virginia C. Groff, John Kathman and LeRoy Whiteman.

Thank you to Michael Dunn for the image from your collection.

And finally, thank you to my family for their support. Special thanks to my husband, John, for unending support and tireless editing skills; my son, Mark, for listening to all the stories and fine-tuning the manuscript;

my brother-in-law Ron for the image from your collection; my sister Carol for your help editing; and to my parents, who were part of the "Greatest Generation." Thank you to my mom, Mary, for encouraging us to step out of the box and to my dad, Fiore, for sharing the stories of his generation and his love of history.

The following pages would not have been possible without the support of everyone listed. I hope the book does justice to the people of Chester County who rose up to take on the challenges the nation faced during the Second World War. The following stories just scratch the surface of the efforts put forth by the industries and communities in the book. And I am sure there are other people, organizations, businesses and stories in the county who contributed to the homefront efforts that are not included in the book. I apologize—there was not enough time or space for this publication alone.

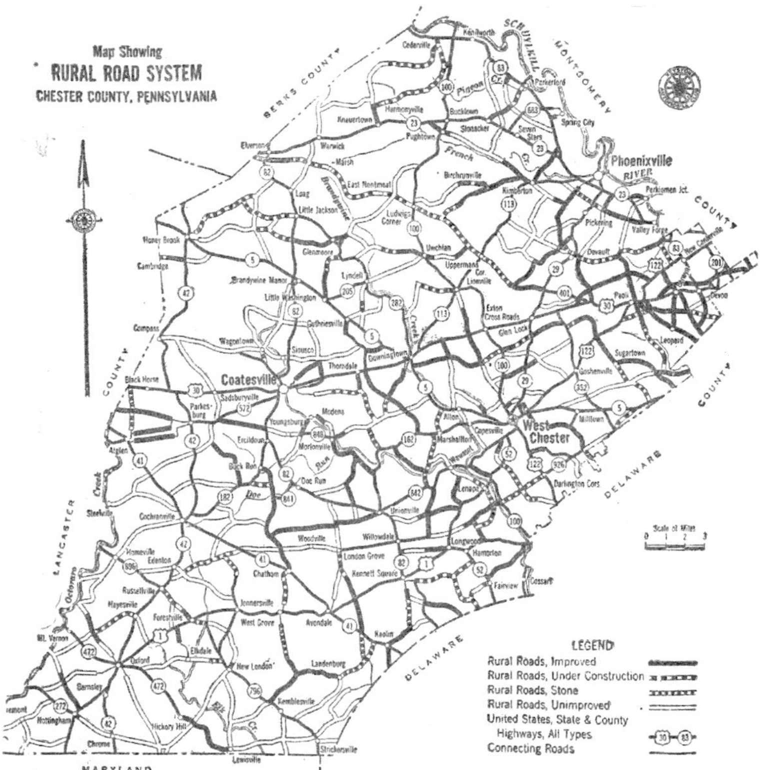

CHESTER COUNTY RURAL ROADS LURE THE SUNDAY DRIVER

THIS map of the rural road system in Chester County was prepared by the Keystone Automobile Club. The heavy lines indicate the improved rural roads, over which motorists may enjoy pleasant week-end driving away from the congestion of main highways. The total mileage of rural highways in the county is 567 miles, of which 311 miles are improved.

July 7 '32.

Local 7.7.1932

A map of Chester County, July 1932. *Chester County Historical Society, West Chester, PA.*

1
Chester County

Chester County is located in southeastern Pennsylvania, west of Philadelphia. It was one of the three original counties founded in 1682 by William Penn, a Quaker who was seeking freedom in North America from religious persecution. King Charles II of England repaid a loan from Penn's father by granting an area of land in America to William after his father's death. Although William Penn was a Quaker, he also welcomed people from other faiths, and as a result, there were immigrants from other parts of Europe who settled in what became known as Pennsylvania.[1] As the nation grew, so did the county. Chester County, an area of rolling hills, thick forests and streams, had mineral-rich soil perfect for farming and raw material that was vital for industry. The county was predominantly rural, but there were pockets of industrial development in towns throughout the county that took advantage of the natural resources and the expanding network of railroads and roads. In addition, as transportation became more accessible, it was easier for residents to travel greater distances from home, so some parts of the county became commuter communities for people who worked in Philadelphia and wanted to live in a more rural setting.

In 1940, Chester County had a population of 135,626, 61 percent rural (82,284) and 39 percent urban (53,342) according to the 1940 census. Though it was more rural than urban, there were mills and manufacturing plants throughout the county that were destined to take on new roles as World War II approached.

2

Buildup to War

Long before the United States entered World War II, there were events around the world that pointed to the eventuality of war. In the 1930s, Japan seized Manchuria from China, and Italy invaded Ethiopia. In 1933, Adolf Hitler became chancellor of Germany. He then violated the Treaty of Versailles and remilitarized the Rhineland.

In the late 1930s, Hitler continued to expand his reach, annexing Austria and marching into Czechoslovakia. Then in 1939, he invaded Poland. In response, Britain and France declared war. Germany formed an alliance with Italy and Japan, and they became the Axis nations fighting the Allied forces.[2] After war was declared, the Allies quickly learned that the Germans had superior planes, tanks and submarines since they had been modernizing their military for years. Great Britain and France had not modernized their military since World War I, and as a result, they were fighting with inferior resources. The Allies were playing catch up, and they needed support from the United States to combat the German military. Although the United States proclaimed its neutrality in 1939, President Roosevelt saw the need for the country to support the Allies. The sacrifices citizens made throughout the Depression and the memories of World War I were still fresh in the minds of many, and it would be a challenge to unite the country for yet another world war.

At the time, the United States was still feeling the effects of the greatest economic crises the nation had ever experienced, the Great Depression. This worldwide economic downturn began in 1929 and continued through the 1930s. In the United States, there was a decline in industrial activity, and unemployment was as high as 24.9 percent in 1933.[3] Buying power was reduced, resulting in decreased consumer spending. People could not find work, and homes were lost. The landscape of the country was affected by social changes like shanty towns built by the homeless and mass migration to locations that had job opportunities. Government programs focusing on restoring the economy and helping the unemployed provided some relief but did not end the Depression.

Chester County, Pennsylvania, was primarily a rural area at that time. Living in the county, you were not immune to the Depression and world events. People felt the effects of the depression, some lost their jobs and work was hard to find. News outside the local community was not as accessible as the instant, twenty-four-hour news cycle that is the norm in the twenty-first century. There was no television, Internet, texts or tweets to catch up on the news or stay in touch with family and friends. Instead, you used telegraph services and telephones that, at times, were party lines and wrote letters to keep in touch. News about world events was primarily available through radio, newspapers, newsreels shown at local theaters before feature films and word of mouth. If you could not afford a telephone or radio, there were local newspapers servicing the county's 135,626 residents[4] like the *Downingtown Archive*, the *Coatesville Record*, the *Oxford Press*, the *Daily Local News* and the *Daily Republican*, a Phoenixville newspaper. "Hitler Pushes Way into Poland" headlined the September 14, 1939 issue of the *Daily Local News*. As the war expanded in Europe, local papers included news about the escalation of war overseas. There were also stories about the setup of the national defense here at home, but everyday life of the average citizen of Chester County was not greatly affected. Events happening a world away may have seemed secondary to many people in Chester County.

That began to change as the war continued to expand when Germany invaded France, Belgium and the Netherlands, and Italy invaded Egypt in 1940.[5] Even though the United States had not declared war, the president recognized the potential threat to the nation. In September 1940, the Selective Service and Training Act was passed.[6] The act required men between certain ages to register for the military draft around the country, including Chester County. On October 19, 1940, the local newspaper, the *Daily Republican*, informed the community that the local draft boards in the county held meetings to organize and that they were ready to "go to work" on Monday. This affected anyone who had a family member eligible for the draft. Congress had also been considering a bill to provide military aid to foreign nations, and in March

1941, the Lend Lease Act was passed. The act was a means for providing military aid to foreign countries whose defense the president felt was crucial to the defense of the United States.[7] Although the country did not enter World War II until December 1941, the support the United States provided the Allies before the bombing of Pearl Harbor spurred long-awaited economic growth for the country. Chester Country, like the rest of the nation, was hungry for the business that would be created by the industries that were focusing on meeting the military needs of the Allied forces. In 1940, the country's unemployment rate was 14.6 percent. The economic boost created by increased production related to the war bolstered the job market, and by 1945, the unemployment rate fell to 1.9 percent.[8] While the government focused on supporting the Allies in Europe and preparing the nation, many industries in Chester County responded to the demand for supplies. This resulted in jobs and growth not seen during the Depression. Then on December 7, 1941, Pearl Harbor was attacked, and the course of the nation changed. The next day, President Roosevelt spoke:

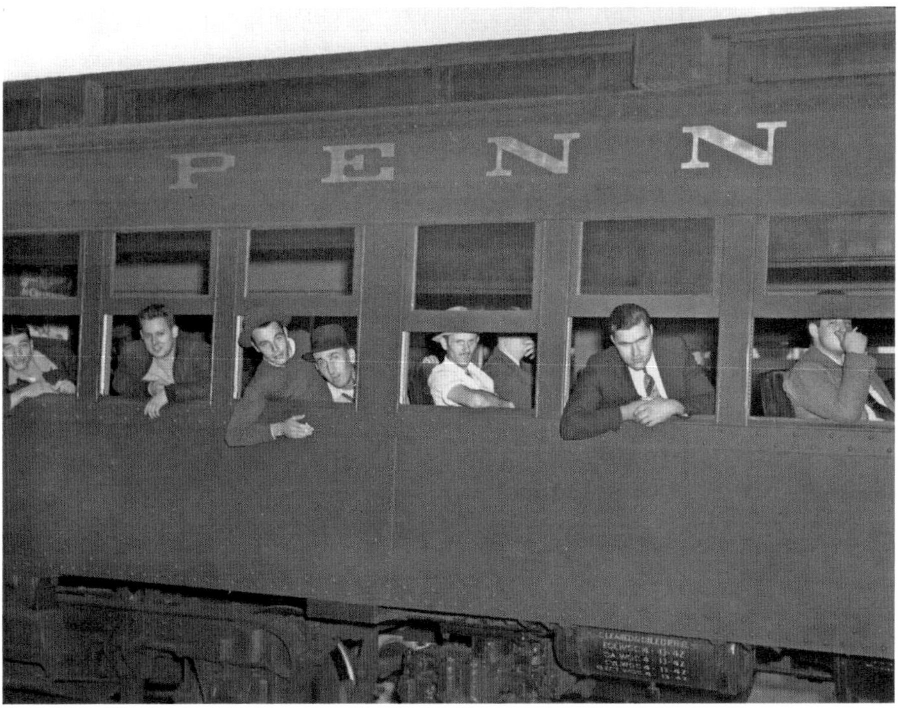

Recruits leaving for war from the West Chester, Pennsylvania Railroad Station, 1942. *Photo by Jimmy John. Chester County Historical Society, West Chester, PA.*

> *With confidence in our armed forces—with the unbounded determination of our people—we will gain the inevitable triumph, so help us God. I, therefore, ask that the Congress declare that since the dastardly and unprovoked attack by Japan on Sunday, December seventh, a state of war has existed between the United States and the Japanese Empire.*[9]

With that proclamation, the United States was officially in the war, and a massive effort to support and mobilize the military from the homefront was underway. To oversee the efforts, there were government agencies, like the War Production Board (WPB), which oversaw war mobilization. The Office of Emergency Management (OEM) was created to coordinate national defense efforts, and the Office of Production Management (OPM) focused on increasing the production of war material and overseeing the distribution of materials for production. Not since the Depression began did so many people have secure jobs and money to spend. Consumers wanted to buy goods, and companies wanted to produce goods for the consumers to buy, but as the nation entered the war, the mobilization effort was a priority.[10] There were numerous obstacles to overcome as industry had to be converted from peace to wartime production, and the material resources necessary for the military buildup had to be found.

The mobilization effort was disjointed and, at times, disorganized, especially in the early stages of the war. The challenges for those who remained at home were numerous. From the creation of jobs to the rationing of resources, daily life was affected. Government production quotes for local industries were demanding to meet wartime needs, there was a shortage of rubber for tires, the sugar supply was reduced and gas was rationed. There was a shortage of workers to replace those who were serving in the military, and as a result, more women entered the workforce for jobs traditionally held by men. In Chester County, the homefront effort was in full swing. There were industries that focused on meeting production demands for military equipment as well as businesses that focused on medical demands like the need for penicillin on the battlefront. Beyond the industrial drive put forth by businesses in the area, the residents of the county made extraordinary efforts to support the war, volunteering for programs like the Red Cross, organizing scrap drives and supporting the troops through organizations such as the YMCA.

Although the efforts were influenced by federal policies, the mobilization of everyday citizens was driven by local communities and individuals in

Chester County. This, in many ways, represented a microcosm of what was happening all over the United States. The following pages tell of the journeys made by many communities and industries around Chester County during the war and reflect the spirit of the people as they met the challenges of a nation at war.

3

Steel Jumps on Board

I have chosen Navy Day, today, to talk about the eleven million Americans in uniform, who with all their strength are engaged in giving us a chance to achieve peace through victory at war. These men could not have been armed and equipped as they are had it not been for the miracle of production here at home. The production which has flowed from the country to all the battlefronts of the world has been due to the efforts of American business, American labor, and American farmers, working together as a patriotic team.

—President Franklin D. Roosevelt, Navy Day speech, October 27, 1944[11]

Lukens Steel Company

Traveling south on Route 82 from Glenmoore, the winding, tree-lined highway crosses Route 30 onto First Avenue in Coatesville, where the Lukens Historic District comes into view. In 1810, Quaker Isaac Pennock and his partner, Jesse Kersey, converted a sawmill into the Brandywine Iron Works and Nail Factory. Isaac eventually became sole proprietor, and after his daughter Rebecca and her husband, Dr. Charles Lukens, moved to Coatesville, Dr. Lukens joined the iron-making business. Under Dr. Lukens's management, they became the first to roll boiler plates in America, and the company's reputation as a manufacturer of high-grade plates supplying shipbuilders and other industries grew. When Dr. Lukens died in 1825, his wife, Rebecca, fulfilled her husband's deathbed request that she continue the business.[12] In the book *Remarkable Past, Promising Future: 200 Years of Iron and Steel Operations in Coatesville, Pennsylvania*, she was described as a "shrewd business manager," and under her leadership, the company continued to grow. Rebecca faced the demands of running a business while raising a family, as well as the additional challenge of being a female in a male-dominated profession. She remained sole proprietor of the company until 1840.[13] The company was incorporated in 1890 as Lukens Iron & Steel Company, and in 1917, the name was changed to Lukens Steel Company. When Isaac Pennock and Jesse Kersey began a business in the early 1800s, they could not have known the impact it would have over one hundred years later during World War II.

During the Second World War, Rebecca Lukens's contributions were recognized when the United States Navy named a Liberty ship the SS *Rebecca Lukens* in 1942. Her leadership was recognized again in the early 1990s when the Pennsylvania legislature, Coatesville and the Chester County Commission named Rebecca Lukens as America's first female industrialist.[14]

The Lukens Steel Company, like most businesses in the country, was affected by the downturn in the economy during the Great Depression as

Constructed in 1902, the Lukens Main Office Building was designed by Philadelphia architects Cope & Stewardson. The building was T-shaped when it opened in 1903. *From the collections of the National Iron & Steel Heritage Museum, Coatesville, PA.*

Rebecca Lukens. *From the collections of the National Iron & Steel Heritage Museum, Coatesville, PA.*

sales as well as job opportunities had declined. This began to change in the early 1940s, as the United States agreed to provide supplies to countries overseas. American industries were anxious for the work and the opportunity for economic growth after the decade-long depression. Steel was one of the things that was in demand, and Lukens Steel found itself positioned to respond to the call for steel production. By 1941, the company's sales increased and income grew, stimulating economic growth for the company as things were getting better. Then on December 7, 1941, the bombing of Pearl Harbor changed the course of the country, and massive mobilization was underway to make sure the nation was in the battle to win. To meet the demand for steel, there was a tremendous effort in Pennsylvania from Bethlehem Steel and the mills in Pittsburgh to pockets of industry in rural areas like Chester County. The results were extraordinary, with Pennsylvania accounting for about one-third of the steel produced in the United States during the war.[15] The secretary of the navy challenged Lukens Steel to meet wartime needs in a telegram. The company's president Robert W. Wolcott's response to the secretary of the navy was published in the company's December 26, 1941 paper, the *Lukens Plate*. He confirmed the support of the "management and the five thousand employees of Lukens Steel Company, By-Products Steel Corporation and Lukenweld, Inc.," saying they would provide steel products "in ever increasing volume because we, like all Americans, remember Pearl Harbor." This was not long after the bombing of Pearl Harbor, and with emotions running high, these words were powerful.

Production

Most people had a family member or knew someone who was serving in the military and wanted to do something to support them from the homefront. The people who worked at Lukens Steel did their part by providing the steel

Liberty ship *Rebecca Lukens*. *From the collections of the National Iron & Steel Heritage Museum, Coatesville, PA.*

that would be used to build equipment for the military buildup. Production quotas were consistently met through the efforts of the Lukens Steel community, and in March 1942, the Navy "E" Award was presented to the company for outstanding production. As the demand grew, the company had the opportunity to expand its output capabilities. In 1942, the navy began construction of a mill that the company leased and operated. The mill was ready for operation by 1943, increasing the company's production capabilities.[16] Employees continued to give their all throughout the war, meeting and, at times, exceeding production quotas.

One of the many uses of Lukens Steel to support the war effort existed within the shipbuilding industry. The government had set aggressive shipbuilding goals for the country. Vessels were needed to replace those that were sunk by German U-boats, or submarines, and to meet the increasing demand for supply ships and troop transports. The Liberty ship program was one of many examples of the tremendous production effort during the war. These ships carried tons of needed cargo and fuel important to the

Navy "E" Award. *From the collections of the National Iron & Steel Heritage Museum, Coatesville, PA.*

military supply chain. During the war, over 2,700 Liberty ships were mass produced, and Lukens Steel products were part of that effort.[17] One of the few Liberty ships that are still operational, the USS *John W. Brown*, has a plaque on board acknowledging Lukens Steel's contributions.[18]

Workforce

Approximately 16 million Americans served in the armed forces during World War II.[19] To keep production going, businesses had to find replacements for those who left for the military. In addition, as companies increased production, there was also a need to expand the existing workforce, which intensified labor shortages throughout the country. Lukens Steel faced these same challenges. Members of the Lukens Steel community worked hard to maintain the tremendous amount of production necessary to keep supplies flowing to the front lines, and as workers left for the armed services, the company was forced to deal with labor shortages to keep up with production.

Employees of Lukens Steel who left the company for the military were guaranteed their job when they returned, but the company had to find replacements for these workers while they were away. In addition, there also

Lady steel workers. *From the collections of the National Iron & Steel Heritage Museum, Coatesville, PA.*

was a need to increase the overall workforce to meet growing production demands; the number of employees at Lukens Steel surged to over six thousand in 1944.[20] One of the company's solutions to the labor shortage was implemented in 1942. In response to labor demands, the company began hiring women to work in the steel division for the first time in its history. A headline in the October 30, 1942 issue of the *Lukens Plate* read, "Greeting Lady Workers." Women who worked at Lukens Steel Company prior to 1942 were limited to office/clerical positions, except for Rebecca Lukens, of course. Now the company was training women for jobs that were traditionally held by men. The story in the paper credited these new employees with meeting demands in the workplace while keeping things going at home as well. This trend was seen across the nation, and from 1940 to 1945, the percentage of female workers in the Unites States workforce increased from 27 to about 37 percent.[21]

Lukens Plate

As in any community, communication is important, and to keep the lines of communication open, the company published a paper called the *Lukens Plate*, which became *Lukens Life* in 1945. It was published "By and For the Employees of Lukens Steel Company, By-Products Steel Corporation, Lukenweld Inc., and their Families."[22] The publication helped connect the world of production to the community life of the company and Coatesville. The *Lukens Plate* included general company updates like credit union news as well as highlights about safety, information about employees and their families, updates and letters from previous employees serving in the military, communications from the president of the company and community events like salvage drives and car sharing programs to support the war effort.

"Chatterbox" was a regular column that included brief bits of information about the Lukens Steel community, much like news sound bites of today. Regardless of where you worked in the company, chances were you knew someone mentioned in the "Chatterbox." The January 21, 1944 issue included news from a former employee stationed on the Pacific Coast as well as a congratulations to newlywed "Lukenites" on their marriage.

Business news could be found in the publication and included information about the company's production efforts, news from the War Department and details of plans to improve the plant. There was also information about

112" Mill Flag Raising

One of the most recent flag raising ceremonies took place at the 112" Mill. The workers took up a collection to buy the flag, which cost $20, and they had $10 left over to send to the Philadelphia Inquirer's "Buy a Bomber" Fund.

One of the United States flags flown throughout the plant, the 112 Mill Flag. *From the collections of the National Iron & Steel Heritage Museum, Coatesville, PA.*

how the company's products were directly impacting the war effort. In the April 3, 1942 issue, a telegram from the War Department described how a brigade of tanks with parts made by By-Products had an "amazing stand" in Libya against two German "panzer divisions." Another article, from February 6, 1942, described an employee campaign around the plant to show support and national pride. The headline read, "Flags Spring up Throughout Plant."[23] United States flags were purchased with money collected by employees. The flags were raised outside the buildings at the mill as a reminder of those serving in lands away from family and friends in Chester County. The number of people serving reported in the January 21, 1944 issue of the *Lukens Plate* was 1,662.

Financing the war was part of the homefront effort, and the *Lukens Plate* had updates about the savings bond program. In September 1942, many employees at Lukens Steel were participating in the bond program—81.5 percent of the workforce purchased bonds.[24] In another issue, five members of a family were commended when they contributed 10.0 percent of their salaries to war bonds.[25] War bond sales were posted in some issues by departments, and there was a companywide "Jingle Contest" that was a creative way to encourage bond sales. The Jingle Contest was open to any employee who was interested in submitting a war jingle. An extra incentive to joining the contest was the twenty-five-dollar defense bond that was awarded each issue for the best jingle.[26]

1810
FIRST TO ROLL BOILER PLATE IN AMERICA

LUKENS PLATE

Published Every Other Week
By and For the Employees of Lukens Steel Company,
By-Products Steel Corporation, Lukenweld, Inc.,
And Their Families

1942
THE WORLD'S LARGEST PLATE MILL

VOLUME 9 — COATESVILLE, PA., JULY 10, 1942 — NO. 14

War Bond Sales Fall Off

Despite the fact that 54 more employees are buying War Bonds now than last pay day, the over-all percentage of purchases for all three companies showed a drop during the last two weeks.

This came about mostly because several hundred new employees were added to our payrolls. Only at Lukens proper did the number of people buying Bonds show an increase. At both By-Products and Lukenweld, some employees stopped purchasing Bonds and very few new names were added to the list of buyers.

Today

Company	Total Employees	Bond Buyers	Pct.
Lukens	3,595	2,527	70
Lukenweld	1,296	816	63
By-Products	678	611	90
	5,569	3,954	71

Last Pay.

Company	Total Employees	Bond Buyers	Pct.
Lukens	3,276	2,398	73.2
Lukenweld	1,171	875	73.2
By-Products	651	627	96.3
	5,098	3,900	76.5

FIGURES TELL THE STORY

True there were a few bright spots in War Bond Sales during the last two weeks. The following Lukens Departments hit the 100 per cent mark: 112" Mill Floor, Universal Mechanical Maintenance, Cladding, Contract Labor and Pipe Shop.

Only Best Dressed Man

Sport fans will recognize Robert Lammey, former Lukens employee, who used to play basketball for Coatesville High. Bob is with the Air Corps at Ft. Benning, Ga. Pretty sure that's a parachute he's wearing.

War bond sales. *From the collections of the National Iron & Steel Heritage Museum, Coatesville, PA.*

The military news that was included in the publication reminded everyone that the paper was not just for employees and retirees. The *Lukens Plate* was also sent to Lukens Steel Company employees serving in various branches of the armed services in different parts of the world. Like a letter from home, those serving could read local news, read updates about co-workers and keep up on things that were happening at the company. The *Lukens Plate* also published the Lukens Honor Roll, which provided updates of co-workers serving in the military. News about those killed in action, missing in action, wounded in action or taken as prisoners of war could be found on the "Our War Casualties" list. In the September 4, 1942 issue, the sad news of the first Lukens casualty, Private George A. Johnson, was published. He was killed in action on August 10, 1942, making the war seem that much closer, especially to employees who knew him or his family. In January 1944, Private Johnson's parents attended the launching of the USS *George A. Johnson*, named in honor of his service. Lukens Steel Company continued to provide support to the Johnsons, who made the trip for the launching as guests of the company.[27] There were updates about the company's service flag, and in the January 21, 1944 issue, the company's new flag had "1,662" blue stars for the number of employees from Lukens who were in the armed forces.[28] This number included six women who were serving with the "WAVES [Women Accepted for Voluntary Emergency Service] and marines." There were six gold stars on the flag to indicate the number of employees who were killed in action. The publication also printed letters from those serving. A theme in many of the letters received was how much those serving enjoyed the *Lukens Plate*. There were letters from both men and women who were writing from different parts of the world—England, South Pacific, Iran as well as camps around the United States. Many expressed gratitude for the publication, saying it helped them to keep in touch. They credited the publication with keeping them informed about friends and co-workers who were working at Lukens Steel and with providing updates on the whereabouts of fellow co-workers who were also serving. Correspondence frequently included accolades for the quality of the paper.

War service flag. *From the collections of the National Iron & Steel Heritage Museum, Coatesville, PA.*

Outside Community

Rationing and salvage drives were part of everyday life in Coatesville, and the employees of the company were a part of these community efforts as well. The company's president, Robert W. Wolcott, who was the chairman of the Scrap Committee of the American Iron and Steel Institute, coordinated scrap drives.[29] The community salvage program in Coatesville, described in chapter 5, was supported by the company, and Lukens Steel also had a salvage committee. Gas rationing limited people's ability to travel, and Lukens Steel encouraged carpooling. The company had a list of employees offering or looking for rides to work. According to the January 1944 issue of the *Lukens Plate*, 3,229 Lukens employees drove to work with the average number of two and a half people per car. Employees were also encouraged to become involved in volunteer activities and in community scrap drives.

The War Ends

Throughout the war, the Lukens Steel community maintained production to support the military effort. The outcome of these efforts was celebrated as joy greeted the end of the war. The company, like the rest of the nation, was ready for peace. In the August 31, 1945 issue of the *Lukens Plate*, Robert W. Wolcott wrote:

> *We fought four long years to preserve our freedom and that of the world from dictators, tyrants and fanatics. How well we, as individuals and as a nation handle our reconversion to peace time pursuits will determine our ability to keep those ideals for which we worked and fought.*

Lukens Steel Company Today

Steel from Lukens Steel can be found in famous structures like the St. Louis Gateway Arch. In the late 1960s, Lukens Steel Company produced the tree beams, or support columns, used in construction of the World Trade Center in New York City. The columns have become an iconic symbol of the terrorist attacks on September 11, 2001, and one of the original beams from the trade center is on display at the National Steel Museum in Coatesville, Pennsylvania. In 1998, the company was acquired by Bethlehem Steel, ending 188 years of independent ownership. Ownership changed again in 2001 and 2003. In 2006, the owner, Mittal Steel, merged with Arcelor to form ArcelorMittal, the present owner, making it a part of a global company with factories in over sixty countries. The company continues to operate plants in Coatesville and Conshohocken, Pennsylvania, today.[30]

PHOENIX IRON COMPANY

The phoenix is a mythical bird that sets itself on fire at the end of its life only to be reborn as a new phoenix. One of the early owners of the iron company, Lewis Wernwag, said the hot iron made him think of the mythical bird, hence the name that, in many ways, represents the company's resilient spirit, which was evident in its contributions to steel production during World War II and throughout its history.[31]

Phoenix Iron Company, located in the northeastern corner of Chester County, was also providing steel as part of the mobilization effort. In the late 1700s, Quaker Benjamin Longstreth bought a gristmill, and on that site, he built the first nail factory in the country. In 1813, Lewis Wernwag purchased part ownership in the business and named it Phoenix Iron Works. Ownership

Phoenix Iron, circa 1944. *Historical Society of the Phoenixville Area, Phoenixville, PA.*

changed again over time, and then in 1827, the mill was sold to the firm of Reeves and Whitaker. This was the beginning of the leadership of the Reeves family that lasted nearly 118 years. The company was incorporated as the Phoenix Iron Company in 1885. The company's history of innovativeness included the manufacturing of the Griffen Gun during the Civil War and the invention of the "first hollow, wrought-iron column" that was used in bridges and buildings around the country. The company's transition to steel began in the mid-1800s.[32] The company continued innovations to modernize and remain competitive among a growing steel industry, and in the 1940s, it was positioned for steel production as part of the mobilization effort during World War II.

Strike

As the war grew in Europe and the United States began supplying the Allies with equipment, steel was needed. It was needed not only to help supply material to the Allied forces but also to modernize the United States military. As a large employer in the community at that time, the economic growth of the company brought growth to the community as well. But then in May 1941, a strike was called that threatened jobs for the local community and the company's viability.

Maury Klein, in *A Call to Arms*, described labor and management disputes during World War II that resulted in work stoppages and strikes.[33] Management and labor at Phoenix Iron Company had to overcome such a division when the strike was called in 1941. The strike began after the CIO's (Congress of Industrial Organizations) request for a "consent election to determine the bargaining agent" was rejected because the company already had an agreement with the employees' association.[34] The strike began on May 14 and picketing started. The Phoenix Iron Company kept the plant open for several days to give employees an opportunity to return to work. Not enough workers took the opportunity, and production stopped. In the meantime, the National Labor Relations Board (NLRB) reviewed and rejected the CIO petition for a consent election. In the local newspaper, the *Daily Republican*, the headline on May 19, 1941, was "Phoenix Iron Company Strike Continues; SWOC Ignore NLRB Ruling," and the plant remained closed. Mill workers were out on strike; only maintenance and office workers were reporting for work. Meetings were held and both sides remained firm, so the strike continued. Then on May 27, during one of President Roosevelt's

Phoenix Iron Company. *Chester County Historical Society, West Chester, PA.*

Phoenix Iron Company. *Chester County Historical Society, West Chester, PA.*

fireside chats, he emphasized how important it was to make sure that the production and transportation of material and equipment needed for the military be uninterrupted by issues on the homefront like disputes between management and labor.[35] In the *Daily Republican*, there was an editorial about the strike the next day. The editorial in the May 28, 1941 issue described the strike as "direct opposition" to the president's comments. During the CIO meeting on May 28, the president of the union told attendees that the strike was called off. That night, some of the 1,400 workers were called back to work. The plant resumed operations as quickly as possible, and everyone was back to work by June 2.[36]

Production

Now that the work stoppage was over, the company was ready for production. As it did during World War I, Phoenix Iron Company ran at full capacity during World War II. Production was in full gear, and the company's output was going into war work. But there were bumps in the road to keep production going. First there was the work stoppage in 1941, in 1942 a flood briefly interrupted production and then the company had to deal with a request from the War Labor Board.[37] In 1942, President Roosevelt set up the War Labor Board, which had the ability to adjust wage levels.[38] In January 1943, the company was notified by the War Labor Board that it had to increase the hourly pay rate of employees. Increasing the price of the product would help meet new payroll demands, but at the time, the federal government set the base selling price for steel. In order to cover the expense of the raise to employees, the company would need "a grant of further price relief," which was complicated since that could make it less competitive.[39] Although it is not clear how the issue was resolved, production continued, and in September 1943, the company was working on thirteen "derrick barges" for the Army Engineers.[40] In February 1944, the same month that company president Samuel J. Reeves was killed in an automobile accident, the company reported record production. This was despite a shortage of manpower. A spokesmen reported, "Virtually the entire credit for the increasing tempo of production is theirs."[41] The new president, David Thomson, took over as the company continued record production. According to an article in the *Daily Republican* on June 6, 1944, the "finishing Mills…established a record production during the month of May, topping that of any other one month in their entire history."[42]

Workforce

The company had to find replacements for the men who left to serve in the military. Like at Lukens Steel, women were hired at Phoenix Iron Company as one way to help meet labor needs. During the war, the female percentage of the workforce in the nation increased. But even with the addition of women to the workforce, labor shortages continued to plague the company.

After the War

In 1944, the era of Reeves leadership of the company ended when President Samuel J. Reeves Jr. died in an automobile accident. Following his death, the company ownership changed before closing in June 1949. But true to its name, like the mythical Phoenix, it rose from the ashes as a new owner bought Phoenix Iron and Phoenix Bridge Company in August 1949. The Phoenix Iron Company became Phoenix Iron and Steel Company. In 1959, Phoenix Iron and Steel Company was eventually renamed Phoenix Steel Corporation. After almost two hundred years of business in the town of Phoenixville, the company closed in 1987.[43]

4

Other Industries Join the Cause

The military needed more than planes, tanks and ships during World War II. It also needed equipment and supplies for all types of operations used in military engagements. Equipment needs ranged from compressors and machine parts to medical supplies and clothing. Here, too, Chester County businesses were part of the supply chain for these goods.

Schramm Inc.

Schramm Inc., headquartered in West Chester, Pennsylvania, produced compressors, generators and other products vital to maintaining military equipment on the front lines during the Second World War. The spirit that helped guide Schramm Inc. through the war years dates back to its founding in 1900, when Christian D. Schramm entered into a business partnership, Schramm & Maerky. The business, which provided gas engine repair, found a market for its services in Philadelphia. After the dissolution of the partnership in 1902, Chris continued the business. In 1907, his son, Henry N. Schramm, became a partner, and the company name was changed to Chris D. Schramm & Son. The company's reputation and business grew, and in 1908, it built the first portable air compressor. The success of the product led to expansion of product lines and the opening of a branch office in New York City. The company's tie to Chester County began in 1917, when it purchased a factory building in West Chester. Then in 1921, the main office was relocated to West Chester, beginning a relationship with the West Chester community that remains today. In 1922, the company's name was changed to Schramm Inc., as it is known today.[44] The pioneer spirit of the company continued throughout the 1920s and 1930s with product development and a workplace that included paid vacations, a life insurance program and sick benefits for employees. Although commonplace today, these benefits were unusual for the time.

A document from the company's records titled "World War II" by Harold J. Schramm described the company's activities related to the war years. Even before the United States entered the war, the government had contacted the company to learn about its production capabilities. At that time, the government had identified products that it felt would be needed in a time of war for different branches of the military. However, the products that the government had identified before the war were not required when the war began. Instead, Schramm Inc. products were manufactured to meet the demands of various departments of the armed forces based on actual wartime needs. Compressors, generators, floodlight trailers and other equipment were shipped to various branches of the military. Even with the push for fast production runs, the company was able to build product variations to meet the requirements specified by different military departments. At the same time, the company was also challenged with requests for production of new equipment. One product order was the navy's request for a small "floodlight trailer." These portable trailers were to be used to light munition igloos (concrete buildings that were used to store weapons and ammunition). The company initially won a contract for a prototype and 200 floodlight trailer units. Later, the company received another contract for over 1,800 floodlight trailers to be used by all branches of the service. Another interesting request that Schramm Inc. received was for the development of a device that would inflate and deflate rubber inflatable boats. The company designed a device that pumped air into rubber boats, or pontoons, that also had the capability to deflate the boats by turning the valve a different direction.[45]

As the United States expanded its military operations around the world, Schramm Inc.'s products traveled with them. In the September 22, 1943 *Daily Local News*, it was reported that four "mobile machine shops from Philadelphia are at the plant of Schramm Inc. today where they are being equipped with electric generators, air compressors and welders" to be sent to the battle front. The mobile units were to be used to make on-site repairs to equipment damaged in battle. This alleviated the need to send

Schramm factory, 1945. *Courtesy of Richard E. Schramm, Schramm Inc.*

Cover of *Schramm INK*, August 1944. The photograph was sent to Schramm Inc. from the United States Navy Department. The caption read "Kwajalein in the Marshalls" and showed a Schramm compressor in the picture. *Courtesy of Richard E. Schramm, Schramm Inc.*

the equipment back to the United States for repair. Doing on-site repairs saved time and money.[46] An often overlooked aspect of the mobilization effort, this equipment was vital to the military. According to a newspaper article in September 1943, "While Schramm does not manufacture guns, ammunitions or other similar equipment, used to destroy our common enemies, it does produce equipment which is used to maintain the guns and the other weapons of war."[47]

Production

Production was key to the mobilization effort, and Schramm Inc. responded to the demand. The company was awarded a Certificate of Honor from the Department of Labor and Industry for the year 1941, and in June 1942, 70 percent of the company's output was being used by the navy and army overseas as the company was "engaged 100 percent on defense orders."[48] As the war progressed and production demands grew, Harold J. Schramm described the "1196 Program" as "one of the highlights" of the war. The company received an ordinance for 1,196 "generators, welders and compressor units." Although they had been working on the ordinance, the time frame was accelerated, and the units had to be completed in just six weeks. The company, responding to what seemed to be an impossible task, launched the project with twenty-four-hour production. There were two twelve-hour shifts for men and three eight-hour shifts for women. Women who were working at the company also saw the female workforce grow quickly as seventy women were hired in three days. At the end of the six weeks, a ceremony was held as the 1,196th unit was loaded for shipment at six o'clock in the morning, on schedule. Employees may not have known why the units were being built or where they would be used, but that did not deter the workforce as they worked seven days a week around the

Cover of *Schramm INK*, October 1942. "War Extra 1196." *Courtesy of Richard E. Schramm, Schramm Inc.*

clock for six weeks.[49] The Schramm Inc. community was part of the drive to meet military needs, and those efforts were acknowledged with a Special Commendation from the United States Marine Corps and the U.S. Navy Certificate of Achievement Award in 1945.[50]

Workforce

As production demands grew, so did the need for skilled workers. Schramm Inc., like other companies, began hiring women for the factory floor. The first women were hired to work in the factory in 1942. The company paper, *Schramm INK*, not only welcomed the women but also made the point that, even though a lot of attention was given to women serving in uniform, women at home were doing their part to support the war effort without the uniform.[51] The company also had to deal with the physical limitations and time restrictions of the plant that limited its production capabilities. It came up with an innovative solution when it announced plans to subcontract work to local businesses that were not involved in war work. For example, while automobile manufacturers changed over to wartime production building bombers, tanks and jeeps, the local car dealerships were impacted as production of new cars slowed down or stopped. Schramm Inc. began using "local but dormant facilities"—such as Sellhast Chevrolet, West Chester Ford, Hoopes Brothers and Darlington buildings, Battan Motor Company and Downingtown Motors, to name a few—to overcome the limitation of space in its plant. A few examples of the subcontracting program included the use of West Chester Ford to work on Ford units that were used to build generators and compressors, Downingtown Motors and Battan Motors providing warehouse space and some subcontractors taking on shipping and packaging.[52]

Schramm INK

As the company grew, it became more difficult for management and personnel to communicate on a regular basis, so *Schramm INK* began in 1942 to keep the lines of communication open. The first issue was published in October 1942, and it was dedicated to those who left for "the active services of the U.S. Army, Navy and Marine Corps."[53] Any employee of Schramm Inc. who was serving in the armed services was automatically put on the

Cover of *Schramm INK*, July 1944. Family Day issue. *Courtesy of Richard E. Schramm, Schramm Inc.*

paper's mailing list. The challenge for the staff at *Schramm INK* was to make sure the publication was delivered to those serving. First, the staff had to confirm that they had the correct address for each person on the list. Then they had to rely on the mail service for delivery, which was not an easy task since the people in the armed services frequently moved from location to location. The staff did their best, as they wrote in the July 1944 issue to the "65 Boys in the Service."

The paper had a variety of material that would appeal to many interests. There were regular columns like "Office Chatter," which included information about employees leaving for military duty, new employees joining the company, birthday wishes and highlights of important events like women joining the workforce. The "From Those in the Service" section shared letters from people in the military. Joseph, a sergeant with the United States marine engineers, wrote in the "Schramm in the Field" column that Schramm's air compressors were an asset to the marines. He went on to say that he felt it was important that people in the factory knew that they were doing a good job.[54] For sports enthusiasts, there were updates in "Sports Chatter" about the company golf championship in 1944 and bowling scores for the men and women who were part of the company's bowling league. Special issues covered important company events like the July 1944 Family Day issue that described the company's first family day picnic. The Christmas issues over the course of the war probably reflected the sentiments of the company, the county and the country. The "Message to Santa Claus" letter in the December 1942 issue read, "Peace is gone and Good Will is hard to find but here among ourselves we have the fires in our hearts that will bring them back." In the December 1945 issue, there were articles like "Again a Peaceful Christmas."

The Schramm community was also part of broader efforts to support the national mobilization as employees participated in the bond program

Cover of *Schramm INK*, July 1943. The Minute Man Flag, Service Man Flag and the United States flag. *Courtesy of Richard E. Schramm, Schramm Inc.*

to help finance the war and made efforts to conserve vital materials. The cover page of the May 7, 1943 issue of *Schramm Ink* published a summary of the bond-buying program at the company. Bond purchases were at 82 percent of the company employees, or 7.8 percent of the payroll. If you had not become part of the bond program, you were encouraged to help the company meet the criteria necessary to earn the Minute Man Flag, a flag that was given to factories when 90 percent of employees gave at least 10 percent of their wages to buy bonds.[55] The company did meet the government criteria for the Minute Man Flag, and the July 1943 cover of *Schramm INK* proudly displayed the Minute Man Flag, the Service Man Flag and the United States flag.

War Ends

When the war ended, the production demands changed as the country adjusted to peace. The August 1945 issue of *Schramm Ink* published portions of the comments made by Henry N. Schramm to workers that month regarding the company's postwar future. He reminded everyone that the company had produced eighteen thousand units during the war. The company was looking forward to finding its place in the postwar world.

Schramm Inc. Today

Today, Schramm Inc.'s headquarters are in West Chester, Pennsylvania. The company manufactures mobile, land-based hydraulic drill rigs sold worldwide for drilling water, oil and gas wells and for mineral exploration.

Schramm Inc. received world acclaim in 2010 for its contribution to the rescue of thirty-three miners trapped for over sixty days in Chili, and in 2013, it received the Governor's Impact Award for exporting.[56]

Penicillin

The historical marker at Walnut and Chestnut Streets in West Chester, Pennsylvania, honors Granville Raymond Rettew, a West Chester native who was instrumental in the production of penicillin during World War II. The marker is a reminder of the tremendous accomplishment that was achieved at the site in the West Chester laboratory.

Today, penicillin is a common antibiotic frequently prescribed by physicians. This was not so during World War II. Although Alexander Fleming discovered penicillin in 1928, the drug was still not available for public use as war approached. The missing link was how to mass-produce penicillin and take the drug from the lab to the patient. When World War II began, research into the mass production of penicillin accelerated since it was believed that the lives of thousands of soldiers wounded in battle could be saved by the drug. Granville Raymond Rettew took on the challenge and was instrumental in the development of a method to mass-produce penicillin.[57]

Rettew was born in West Chester, Pennsylvania, in 1903. His path to working on the production of penicillin was an interesting one. He began

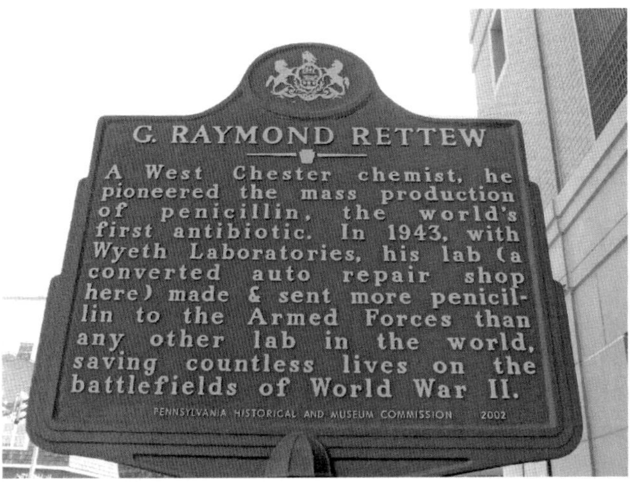

Pennsylvania Historical and Museum Commission street marker, West Chester, Pennsylvania. *Photo by John A. Viglione.*

his studies taking chemistry courses at the University of Delaware and eventually transferred to Swarthmore College, working in the chemistry department as an unpaid assistant. He also worked for a short period of time at his father's law firm before taking a job with a root beer manufacturer. During this time, he became interested in the mushroom industry. His father-in-law worked in the mushroom business, and it was through their conversations that he learned about an issue the industry was facing at the time—poor mushroom spawns (a mushroom spawn is like a seed that is used to propagate mushrooms). Rettew felt that the industry was in need of help, so he and friend and partner Joseph W. Strode opened the Chester County Mushroom Laboratories in West Chester.[58] They worked on "pure cultures of mushroom spawn." Starting a business in the 1930s during the Depression was a gamble, but they were successful. In a few years, sales of the mushroom spawns grew, not just in the United States, but also in other countries like England.[59]

Development

As war approached, Rettew wrote in his memoirs, *A Quiet Man from West Chester*, that he wanted to do his part to support the war effort. First, he knew that if the United States entered the war, there was a strong possibility food would be rationed. As part of a rationing system, certain essential foods would be given priority. Rettew knew that if mushrooms were not considered an essential food, there was a possibility that mushroom growers would be put out of business. So he led an effort by the mushroom industry to determine their nutritional value. The efforts paid off as studies supported the nutritional value of mushrooms, and as a result, mushrooms were listed as an essential food. Rettew then turned to assist in the war effort. Since Chester County Mushroom Laboratories was able "to produce large quantities of pure cultures of fungi," he felt "that work on penicillin would be an ideal project." Penicillin had the potential to save lives, but at that time, there was no way to mass produce the drug for public use. The challenge was great, requiring authorizations from government agencies, laboratory research into the methods of mass production and the development of business relationships to make production a reality. Rettew began studying penicillin in his laboratory. He convinced the chairman of the committee on medical research of the Office of Scientific Research and Development that Chester County Mushroom Laboratories could work for the program.

Since he was not familiar with the pharmaceutical field, he also had to find a company who knew the field. He found such support from John Wyeth and Brother Incorporated, a subsidiary of American Home Products Corporation at that time who agreed to "cooperate in the study." Rettew began working on the production of penicillin in his West Chester laboratory. The first technical assistant joined the team in January 1943, and by the end of June 1943 the first penicillin was sent to the United States Government.[60]

Production

The production process was complicated and had multiple steps. After the solution was made in West Chester, the next step was to dehydrate the "raw" penicillin. Reichel Laboratories in Kimberton had the facility to dehydrate the penicillin. The solution "was 'freeze-dried' and the water was evaporated which left a dry powder penicillin." The arrangement was to

Desmond Biel and G. Raymond Rettew in the air-conditioned room. *Chester County Historical Society, West Chester, PA.*

The building renovated to become the Walnut Street Laboratory, Walnut Street, West Chester, Pennsylvania, circa 1943. *Chester County Historical Society, West Chester, PA.*

make the concentrated solution in West Chester and then ship the solution in refrigerated vehicles to Reichel Laboratories in Kimberton. There, the penicillin was freeze-dried and packaged for shipment.[61]

The original laboratory in West Chester had been expanded, but it soon became apparent that a larger space was need. A garage on Walnut Street, the Pennsylvania Garage, was rented and converted into a penicillin plant where "32,000 surface cultures a day" could be produced. Rettew also gave credit to the town of West Chester when he said that it had many dedicated men and women working "around the clock" who played an important role in the breakthrough of the mass production of penicillin.[62]

After the War

Rettew stayed at Wyeth after the war and did not return to the mushroom industry.[63] During a visit to Philadelphia in 1945, Alexander Fleming was quoted in the August 5, 1945 *Philadelphia Inquirer* as saying:

It isn't exaggerating to say that G. Raymond Rettew beat the whole world at the work of producing penicillin in more than laboratory quantities. Countless men wounded on European battlefields are alive today who would have died save for the first shipments made here under his directions and rushed overseas.

NATIONAL FOAM INC.

James Boyd. *Courtesy of National Foam Inc., West Chester, PA.*

Fisher Boyd. *Courtesy of National Foam Inc., West Chester, PA.*

National Foam Inc. is located in West Chester, Pennsylvania. James Boyd founded the company in Boston in 1819. At that time, he saw that the water coming from fire engines had limited range and pressure. Seeing a need for more sophisticated firefighting equipment, he started a company in Boston manufacturing fire hoses. In 1821, he received the first United States patent for improvement of a fire hose. The patent was signed by the president at the time, James Monroe. The company continued to manufacture firefighting equipment, and the business eventually moved to Philadelphia. Over the years, the business expanded its product line and became a leader in manufacturing fire protection equipment. In the early 1900s, the business was incorporated as National Foam System Inc.[64]

World War II

In the early 1900s, as the use of flammable liquids was growing around the world, so was the possibility of flammable liquid fires. As a result, firefighting material for flammable liquid fires became even more important. Since gasoline and oil fires were frequent

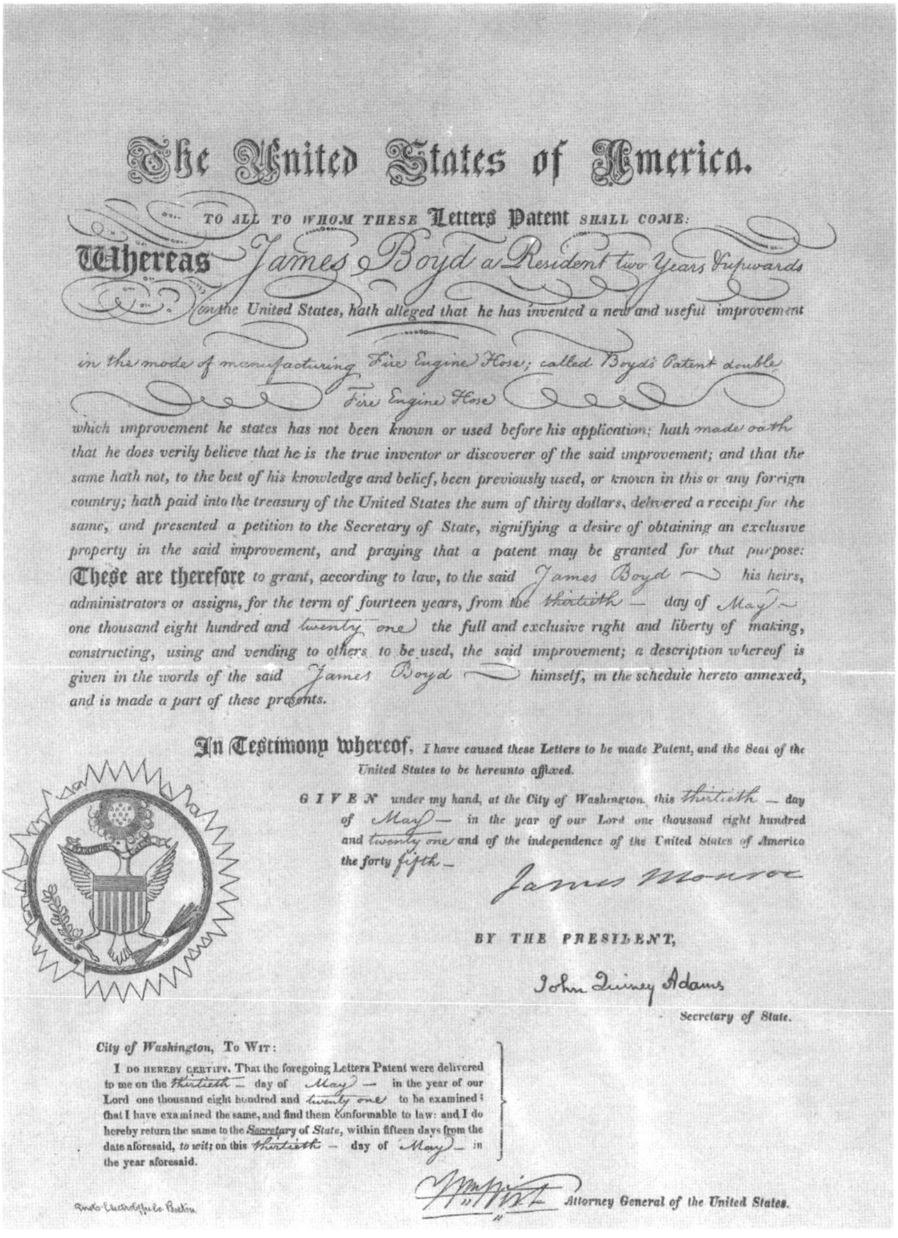

The United States of America.

TO ALL TO WHOM THESE Letters Patent SHALL COME:

Whereas James Boyd a Resident two Years & upwards in the United States, hath alleged that he has invented a new and useful improvement in the mode of manufacturing Fire Engine Hose; called Boyd's Patent double Fire Engine Hose

which improvement he states has not been known or used before his application; hath made oath that he does verily believe that he is the true inventor or discoverer of the said improvement; and that the same hath not, to the best of his knowledge and belief, been previously used, or known in this or any foreign country; hath paid into the treasury of the United States the sum of thirty dollars, delivered a receipt for the same, and presented a petition to the Secretary of State, signifying a desire of obtaining an exclusive property in the said improvement, and praying that a patent may be granted for that purpose: These are therefore to grant, according to law, to the said James Boyd his heirs, administrators or assigns, for the term of fourteen years, from the thirtieth day of May one thousand eight hundred and twenty one the full and exclusive right and liberty of making, constructing, using and vending to others to be used, the said improvement; a description whereof is given in the words of the said James Boyd himself, in the schedule hereto annexed, and is made a part of these presents.

In Testimony whereof, I have caused these Letters to be made Patent, and the Seal of the United States to be hereunto affixed.

GIVEN under my hand, at the City of Washington, this thirtieth day of May in the year of our Lord one thousand eight hundred and twenty one and of the independence of the United States of America the forty fifth.

James Monroe

BY THE PRESIDENT,

John Quincy Adams

Secretary of State.

City of Washington, To Wit:

I DO HEREBY CERTIFY, That the foregoing Letters Patent were delivered to me on the thirtieth day of May in the year of our Lord one thousand eight hundred and twenty one to be examined; that I have examined the same, and find them conformable to law: and I do hereby return the same to the Secretary of State, within fifteen days from the date aforesaid, to wit; on this thirtieth day of May in the year aforesaid.

Wm. Wirt

Attorney General of the United States.

A patent to James Boyd signed by President James Monroe and John Quincy Adams, secretary of state. *Courtesy of National Foam Inc., West Chester, PA.*

byproducts of bombs and other weapons of war, as war grew in Europe, the navy had an increased interest in fire-extinguishing products to fight these fires. The need for new mechanical foam became more urgent as the navy was interested in a system that was "less cumbersome" than what was required to make chemical foam. At that time, there was a mechanical foam product that was being used in Europe, but the company decided to begin work on the development of a mechanical foam that had improved firefighting capabilities. The program resulted in the development of a liquid that included soybeans as a source of one of the ingredients. This new foam was nicknamed "Navy Bean Soup" by the navy, but its official name was "National Aer-O-Foam."[65] In an interview with the author, LeRoy Whiteman, who worked at National Foam Inc. from 1948 to 1993, recalled that a shortened version, "Aer-O-Foam," was the company's in-house name for the mechanical foam product. He also noted that Aer-O-Foam "dissipates easier" than chemical foam. This was a big advantage for customers.

The company successfully delivered the product to the Navy Materials Testing Laboratory for testing before Pearl Harbor was attacked. It passed the Navy's tests, and when the United States entered World War II, the demand for Aero-O-Foam to combat fires accelerated. The foam liquid was initially made at the company's New Jersey facility, but as demand increased, National Foam System Inc. opened a plant in West Chester, Pennsylvania, to produce the new foam. A plant was built in 1942 on East Union Street.[66] By 1943, it was operating twenty-four hours a day.[67] By August of that year, over "1,000,000 gallons of Navy bean soup" had been produced at the West Chester facility.[68]

The twenty-four-hour workday paid off, and high production standards were rewarded in November 1943 when National Foam System Inc. received an Army-Navy "E" Production Award for excellence in war production.[69] *The Army-Navy Production Award Manual*, provided by the Navy Department and the War Department, stated that all plants that were engaged in "war production and construction work for the Army and Navy" were eligible for the production award. When the company was selected to receive the award, an award ceremony was planned closely adhering to the plans in the manual. The booklet included information on the type of equipment needed for the ceremony, speakers and publicity. There was also a detailed schedule for the ceremony—"A time limit of thirty minutes for the entire program should be set and strictly adhered to."[70] The ceremony was held at the West Chester facility as a special train chartered by the company brought workers from the Philadelphia plant to join fellow workers in West Chester.

LeRoy Whiteman applying foam with an air aspirating "PC-31" foam nozzle. *From LeRoy Whiteman's National Foam Collection.*

The original National Foam Inc. plant in West Chester. *Courtesy of National Foam Inc., West Chester, PA.*

A program cover for the Army-Navy "E" Production Award ceremony. *Courtesy of National Foam Inc., West Chester, PA.*

Anyone who attended the ceremony on November 30, 1943, gathered with the crowd in a large heated tent outside the West Chester plant. The ceremony was led by the presiding judge for Chester County Courts, Honorable W. Butler Windle. Guest speaker Rear Admiral T.J. Keleher praised the company's efforts saying, "In West Chester there is the soul of America…The people of West Chester and particularly the workers of National Foam are the workers on which the boys are depending." In that same speech, he described how valuable the foam produced by National Foam had been in saving lives and ships like the *Enterprise*. Employees came together to watch the president of the company, Fisher L. Boyd, accept the pennant for the company as he gave credit to the hard work and efforts of all the workers, saying they were the people who deserved the credit.[71]

Over the course of the war, National Foam System Inc. excelled and received three additional citations for its production record. During the author's interview with LeRoy Whiteman, he recalled that the company received four awards during the war years.

Other products made at the company's various facilities were also used by different branches of the armed services during the war.[72]

On the Front Lines

Hearing about the uses of Aer-O-Foam on the battle lines was inspiring, especially if you worked at the company. In an article in the *Daily Local News* on June 18, 1943, company executive Fisher L. Boyd, who was speaking at a local event, shared a story that exemplified the importance of mechanical foam. He stated that early one morning, he received a telephone call at 2:00 a.m. from someone at the Philadelphia Airport who asked if he could arrange a rush shipment of foam to the airport. The shipment was arranged through the plant foreman, and the product was shipped. Several weeks later, a government official complimented the company on the service it

An advertisement in a trade publication, "Foam Fought Kamikazes—and Won!" *Courtesy of National Foam Inc., West Chester, PA.*

provided, explaining that the foam was quickly shipped that night to the Pacific Coast and then flown to Pearl Harbor. The foam was then transferred to a fireboat that was dispatched to a ship that was on fire "somewhere in the Pacific." The ship was saved because of the efforts of National Foam. Foam equipment made at National Foam System Inc. was also used to put out a fire on a tanker off the shores of Norfolk. The tanker, which was carrying aviation fuel, collided with a munitions ship. The foam helped to save not only the tanker but also 75 percent of its cargo. The article went on to say that because of the success of the equipment, it was being used in all of the navy's firefighting schools.[73] At the end of the war, a company publication stated, "National is now ready to serve industrial organizations and fire departments throughout the world with the best and most exhaustively tested foam of any type ever developed."[74]

National Foam Inc. Today

Today, National Foam Inc. continues to be a leader in the development of innovative firefighting technology with customers in over one hundred countries around the world. National Foam Inc. is headquartered in West Chester, Pennsylvania.

Downingtown Manufacturing Company

Downingtown Manufacturing Company did not produce steel for the hull of a ship or generators to be used on the beaches of the Pacific, but it was as vital to the supply link. During World War II, the company, which was located on Washington Avenue in Downingtown, found itself positioned to provide a variety of parts and equipment to industries that were producing supplies and weaponry for the war.

The history of Downingtown Manufacturing Company dates back to 1880 when A.P. Tutton; his son in-law Guyon Miller; and Guyon's brother, Frank Miller, started the company. The plant on Washington Avenue grew, and production included small steam engines, castings and paper mill machinery.[75] Although the company closed in 1971, its contributions to the war effort can be found in copies of the company's newspaper, *DMC News*. The papers provide a window into the production and spirit of the company as part of the mobilization effort.

Wartime Production

Downingtown Manufacturing Company, like most industries during the war, felt the effects of labor shortages as men left to join the military. Many women were hired to work at the company at that time to overcome workforce shortages. The company produced castings for buoys, sold machinery to manufacturers who produced ration tokens[76] and produced a variety of other products chronicled in the company's newspaper, *DMC News*.

In the July 1943 issue, an article described how tank turret rings were being produced in preparation for the invasion of Europe. The tank turret ring assembly, which required three rings, allowed the turret—the top part of the tank where guns are mounted—to turn easily and quickly to direct fire from the gun. If you served on the crew of a tank, the ability to aim the tank's gun was crucial to survival. It was reported that 13,188 tank rings were made by the company during the Second World War.[77]

The January 1944 issue included an article that credited the company with selling the Downingtown Suction Rolls to Scott Paper Company. The Scott Paper Company developed a tissue that was used to clean the lens of periscopes and other instruments that were equipped with lenses or reflectors. With the help of the Downingtown Suction Rolls, Scott Paper Company produced another paper product, "paper-wipes," which were used as a paper substitute for rags.

According to the March/April 1946 issue, during the war, the company provided equipment to synthetic rubber plants. Rubber was one of the vital resources that was controlled by the Axis powers. As a result, supplies were cut off to the Allies, which caused a shortage of rubber. To overcome these shortages, the production of synthetic rubber increased in the United States during the war. In 1942, 3,721 tons were produced, compared to 756,042 tons produced in 1945.[78] As production increased, so did the demand for equipment to run the plants. Employees of Downingtown Manufacturing Company were part of the synthetic rubber supply chain since the company produced "five, forty-two-inch cast chrome molybdenum butterfly valves" that were used in the manufacturing of synthetic rubber. Parts such as these were part of the production process that kept synthetic rubber flowing.

An article in the May/June/July 1946 issue described how the company produced 10,779 PT (patrol torpedo) boat rings during the war. Similar to the tank turret rings, three rings were necessary for one assembly. Without the assembly, it was difficult to aim the guns since the rings were necessary for "quick sidewise movement" of the gun. Escape hatch covers were also manufactured at Downingtown Manufacturing Company. These hatches were installed under the tank operators. The escape doors opened, providing an emergency exit for the crew.

Downingtown Manufacturing Company also provided the machinery for many paper mills, and paper was a vital resource during the mobilization. Shipping food to those overseas was a priority, but not many thought about how that food would be shipped. This is where paper entered the scene, since most food was shipped to troops in cardboard boxes. In addition, paper was also used as a liner, and things were wrapped in paper.

DMC News

In addition to reporting on production, *DMC News* kept the Downingtown Manufacturing Company community connected. A "Safety Committee Report" and a section with tips to keep your work space safe were regular features. The column "Shop Gossip" was true to its name, sharing short bits of information about co-workers as well as stories about events. Issues also included a column with employee suggestions about the workplace, called "Constructive Thinking." You could catch up on the bowling league in "Bowling Standings" to see how the Shop League and the Industrial League were doing. "Our President's Corner" featured a letter written by the company's president. The content of each letter usually reflected on

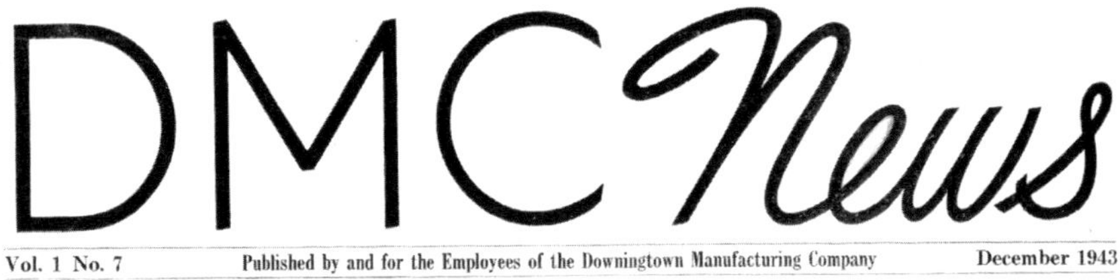

DMC News

Vol. 1 No. 7 Published by and for the Employees of the Downingtown Manufacturing Company December 1943

Downingtown Manufacturing Company newspaper, December 1943. *Used with permission from the General Archival Collection of the Downingtown Area Historical Society, Downingtown, PA.*

current events. In the February 1944 issue, he expressed his gratitude for the effort put forth by employees. He wrote, "It's a hard grinding task to work seven days a week but I know it was a source of satisfaction to all of us to exceed our anticipated shipment as we did on the Navy and other war orders." The company's commitment to the national mobilization effort was visible in its actions. Employees were encouraged to participate in the bond program, and a summary of bond purchases could be found in the paper. In June 1943, the paper included a chart that showed the percentage of participation by departments in the bond program. The percentage for the five departments listed were all 90 percent or greater. Every month, *DMC News* was mailed to everyone serving. There was even a "Who's Where" column that listed the names and addresses of those serving so co-workers could write to them. "Letters from the Boys in the Service" was in another section of the paper. The letters from the people in the armed services often spoke of the newspaper and what it meant to them. For example, one soldier wrote that *DMC News* helped keep people informed about things at home. Others also wrote to thank the editor for the issues of the paper they received.[79]

The 1946 issues of *DMC News* reflected on products the company contributed to the war effort, pointing out that during the war, everyone was focused on working on production, and there was not much time to reflect on how much was accomplished by the company's efforts. The summaries provided in the 1946 issues reviewed different products that were manufactured during the war along with the number of units produced. The first issue of that year was dedicated to former employees who lost their lives during the war and employees who served in the military.

Memorial honoring employees of Collins and Aikman who served in the military during World War II. *From the collection of Michael J. Dunn Sr.*

Downingtown Manufacturing Company Today

After the war, Downingtown Manufacturing Company continued to grow. Ownership changed in 1955, and it was eventually sold again to Beloit Iron Works in Wisconsin. The company continued operations as Beloit Eastern until it closed in 1971.[80]

Collins & Aikman Corporation

The Collins & Aikman Corporation was located on Bondville Road in East Brandywine Township. The company also played a part in the industrial mobilization effort in the county during the Second World War. The remains of what was once the Collins & Aikman plant are now part of Bondsville Mill Park in East Brandywine Township.

The site of the Collins & Aikman plant was the location of a number of gristmills in the 1800s. In 1842, Abraham Bond opened a textile factory. The mill became known as the Bondsville Mill, and a small community built up around the mill. Ownership changed over time, and then in 1927, the property was bought by the Collins & Aikman Corporation. The company opened a plant making upholstery for automobiles. It also provided employment for local residents. During World War II, the plant continued to be operated by Collins & Aikman. It was reported that the company produced the linings for air force jackets.[81] Little information remains about the workforce or production, but a memorial that was built to honor World War II veterans who served still stands today.[82]

Today

After Collins & Aikman closed, the property was used by other businesses until it close, permanently in the 1960s. In 2004, the mill property and surrounding area were purchased by East Brandywine Township. Today, the site is part of the Bondsville Mill Park, which is now open to the public, and remains of some of the mill buildings are still visible as you walk through the park.[83]

5
Communities Chip In

"Do your part" and "we are all in it together" may sound like clichés, but they represented the spirit of the homefront during the Second World War. Regardless of age, race, ethnicity, sex, religion or political affiliation, everyone felt the effects of the war. It didn't matter if you were a supporter of the war, a conscientious objector, a child or an adult—government policies were implemented to make sure the military had what it needed. Tanks, ships, guns and other military equipment were produced at record rates, and providing the armed services with food, clothing and other supplies became a priority. The challenge was to find the resources necessary to support the mobilization effort as well as those at home. A cup of coffee or a new pair of boots didn't seem like too much to sacrifice to make sure the military had what it needed to fight the war.

Rationing

Food

What better way to enjoy friends and family than sitting down for a meal or talking over a cup of coffee? These routines took on new meaning during the war in communities around Chester County. Sending food to those overseas was the priority, so everyone at home had to share what remained. Multiple factors affected the food supply chain on the homefront. Food was being shipped to the troops overseas, and due to the war, food imports were limited. In addition, transportation of fresh food was affected by gasoline and tire shortages. To help deal with these shortages, the government took steps to prevent out-of-control price increases and to come up with an equitable system of distribution of foods. In 1942, the Office of Price Administration set price limits and established a rationing system for certain foods.[84] Imported foods like sugar and coffee were rationed, as well as products like cooking oil, meat and canned goods. Ration books were issued, and a ration stamp or coupon had to be used to buy rationed foods. Each food item was given a value or a number of points by the government. In addition to stamps, tokens were also used beginning in 1944, which made it easier to give change. Only the person or family who had applied for the ration book could use the stamps in that book.[85]

Individuals and families adjusted to the rationing system. For example, during an interview with the author, Margaret B. Chalfant, a resident of Chester County during the Second World War, recalled that rationing coupons could be used in any store and her family also

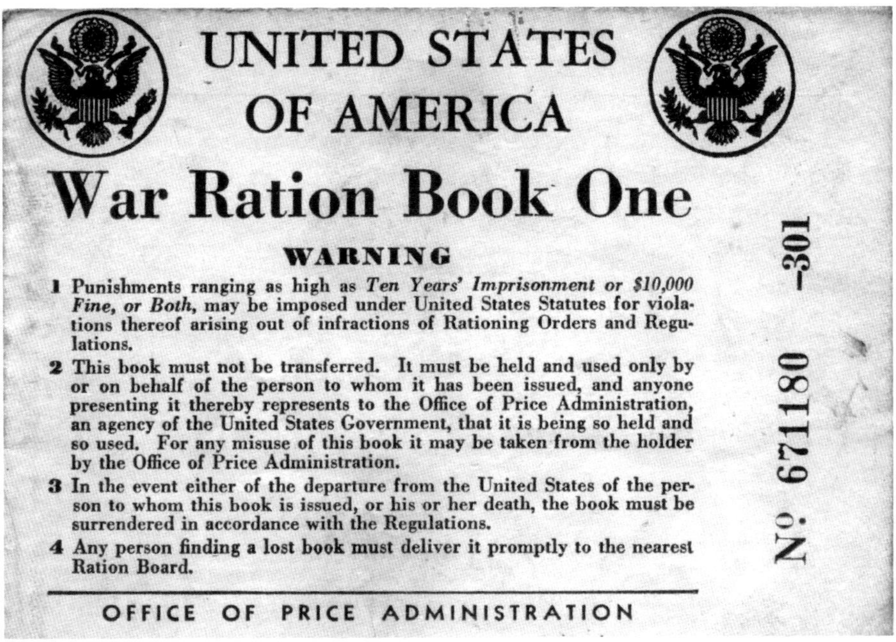
UNITED STATES OF AMERICA

War Ration Book One

WARNING

1 Punishments ranging as high as *Ten Years' Imprisonment or $10,000 Fine, or Both,* may be imposed under United States Statutes for violations thereof arising out of infractions of Rationing Orders and Regulations.

2 This book must not be transferred. It must be held and used only by or on behalf of the person to whom it has been issued, and anyone presenting it thereby represents to the Office of Price Administration, an agency of the United States Government, that it is being so held and so used. For any misuse of this book it may be taken from the holder by the Office of Price Administration.

3 In the event either of the departure from the United States of the person to whom this book is issued, or his or her death, the book must be surrendered in accordance with the Regulations.

4 Any person finding a lost book must deliver it promptly to the nearest Ration Board.

No. 671180 -301

OFFICE OF PRICE ADMINISTRATION

A war ration book. *Chester County Historical Society, West Chester, PA.*

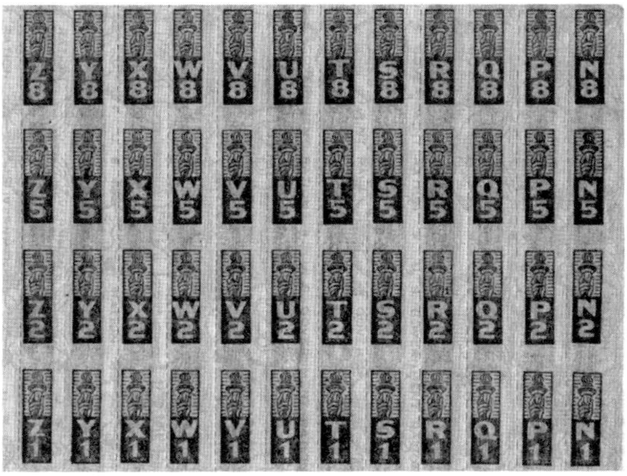

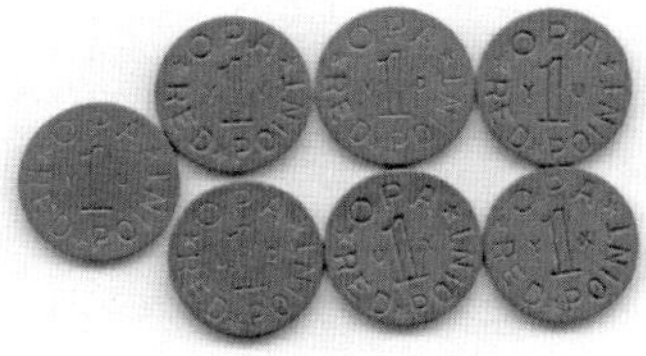

Above: Red ration tokens. *Chester County Historical Society, West Chester, PA.*

Left: Rationing stamps. *Used with permission from the General Archival Collection of the Downingtown Area Historical Society, Downingtown, PA.*

grew food on their farm, which helped during the rationing program. The rationing system did not allow for trading, selling or giving away of stamps, so you could only purchase the amount of food allotted by your stamps. You could not purchase additional ration stamps from the government or buy stamps from friends or neighbors, although a black market for some rationed items was reported. Grocery shopping and planning for a special meal to celebrate a holiday or special event were challenges.

Rationing was not the only plan for addressing food shortages. There were campaigns to encourage citizens to conserve, and victory gardens were promoted around the country. People who lived on one of the many farms in Chester County at the time were fortunate, since they had access to fresh produce. People who did not live on a farm had the opportunity to plant a victory garden. Some schools planted gardens on school property, and there were people who did not have a yard who planted a few things where they could, like in window boxes. During the war, millions of gardens were planted, and in 1944, 40 percent of the vegetables grown in the United States were from victory gardens. A bonus to planting a victory garden was that extra food from the garden could be canned so that it could be used during the winter months.[86] Growing vegetables was encouraged and even became a social event like at the Junior Fair in West Bradford Township that was held on August 25, 1943. The event took place at the Marshallton school at 2:00 p.m. The flyer read, "West Bradford Township Junior Fair to be held Under the Auspices of the U.S. Citizens Service Corps." If you were under eighteen years of age and lived in West Bradford or if you attended West Bradford schools, you were eligible for the events. Adults were also invited to attend

Earl Hutton in his victory garden in West Chester, Pennsylvania, 1942. *Photo by Jimmy John. Chester County Historical Society, West Chester, PA.*

the free event to see the displays. The fair included a Victory Garden Show. Each child who participated in the Victory Garden Show was asked to bring no more than three vegetables from his or her garden or the family vegetable garden. The plates for display of the vegetables were to be provided, and a judge selected the winner. Contestants had the opportunity to win awards for the best exhibit of "each kind of vegetable, the tallest stalk of corn, the largest tomato, and the greatest variety from any one garden." The fair also included contests for canned goods, flower arrangements and baked goods. There was a poster contest, and children were also encouraged to bring arts and craft projects they made that summer to display.[87] Retailers also responded to the trend for gardening. In the April 1942 issue of the *Main Line Caller*, put out by Strawbridge & Clothier, there was an advertisement for a new line of clothing for gardeners. Illustrations enticed buyers to consider garments like denim slacks and women's "chambray overalls." The overalls had pockets, and there was a place to "insert rubber knee-pads for kneeling," which made it more comfortable when working in the garden. Garden gloves were also available for one dollar. In addition to clothing, the store also advertised garden tools that were available on the lower floor of the store.[88]

Gasoline

Tires, shoes, kerosene and gasoline were just a few of the other items rationed during World War II. Fuel for tanks, ships, planes and other military equipment was a priority, and gasoline rationing at home became part of the plan to meet those demands. In addition, there was a shortage of rubber, and rationing gasoline would help limit travel and conserve rubber that could be used for the military. The challenge was to make sure that emergency workers and people who worked in war-related plants had what they needed to run the plants and get to and from work while at the same time considering the energy needs of other citizens. Like the food rationing program, everyone was affected by the gasoline rationing program. But the system was different than the food rationing program. Gasoline ration stamps were distributed by local boards based on travel needs. The stamps were displayed in the windshield of automobiles, and the allotment of gasoline was based on the type of stamp a person was issued. Most people qualified for an A sticker, which was three to four gallons per week. Defense workers and emergency personnel qualified for more gasoline.[89] Margaret B. Chalfant recalled that she and her husband were eligible to apply for additional gas coupons since she was a member of the Red Cross and her husband was in the medical profession. However, they did their part to conserve and were careful about their travel so they never had to apply for additional gas coupons. At work, people were encouraged to carpool and participate in other conservation efforts. Even students at colleges and universities in Chester County felt the effects of gas rationing since they had restrictions on the use of the family car for commuting to and from school.

Salvage Efforts

As the war progressed, the need for raw material to meet industrial production quotas increased. On the homefront, there were reminders of the need for vital material for the war effort everywhere. At work, people were reminded to save rags and were encouraged to car pool. At home, the local newspapers encouraged everyone to join the cause by donating unnecessary utensils or other metal. The Department of Agriculture even published a pamphlet encouraging farmers to gather scrap metal around the farm. During the war, the federal government helped organize and promote scrap drives for vital materials, and communities as well as groups like the Boy Scouts had scrap drives.

Coatesville Salvage Campaign

Coatesville organized the Coatesville Salvage Campaign during the war. The pamphlet *Salvage* provided a detailed description of the program.[90] A letter on the inside cover was written by the president of Lukens Steel Company, Robert W. Wolcott. He emphasized the importance of salvage and reminded everyone of the material shortages the industry was facing. He encouraged everyone to participate, and he closed the letter saying that he hoped the information in the pamphlet might help others organize campaigns in their communities.

The "Cleanup Week" scrap drive, as described in *Salvage*, was a plan that was implemented by the city of Coatesville, and organization seemed to be key to the plan. The mayor of Coatesville appointed a chairman of the Salvage Committee. The chairman then appointed chairpersons for seven committees, ranging from entertainment and publicity to demolition.

According to the publication, once the plan was in place, the mayor made an announcement in the *Coatesville Record*, the local paper. The city's "annual clean up week" would be combined with the Salvage Committee campaign from April 13 to 18.[91] The following week, the salvage committee ran paid advertisements that informed people of the campaign and encouraged everyone to participate. Movie theaters in Coatesville showed advertisements about the campaign. In addition, businesses in the city put posters about the campaign in their windows, and a large banner hung across Lincoln Highway. The publicity committee did not stop there; there was a sound truck that drove through the city during the day for a few hours before and during the campaign. The truck played music and reminded everyone to participate in the salvage drive. If you lived in Coatesville, you had to have seen or heard an advertisement about the drive.

The canvassing committee began to visit homes and business establishments in Coatesville. The Ladies of Coatesville Chapter of the American Red Cross was the group responsible for going to homes to ask residents to participate in the campaign and look for any available salvage materials that they may have to donate to the drive. If a person had salvage materials for the collection, the person was given a window sticker to display. The sticker identified homes that were contributing to the campaign. The chamber of commerce and the Coatesville Council of Defense visited businesses as well as industries like garages in Coatesville. If they participated in the drive, they also received a sticker to display in their windows.

With everything in place, the next step was collection of the scrap. There were multiple collection options available to meet the needs of just about any donor who had scrap to donate:

1. Call a city-owned truck to pick up the donation from homes or business.
2. Take scrap metal and other salvage items to the Victory Scrap Yard.
3. If you had large scrap that you could not remove yourself, you could contact the Salvage Committee Demolition Crew. The crew would cut the metal up and then take it to the scrap yard.

The Victory Scrap Yard was the site for the collection. The scrap yard was located on Lincoln Highway where a vacant lot was sectioned off and became the area for the collected salvage. Banners and interesting items that were donated to the scrap yard were put up outside the yard to get the attention of people passing by the area. At night, there were floodlights set up to illuminate the scrap yard. There was also a scoreboard that kept track of the amount of scrap collected. A photograph in *Salvage* showed an image of tanks on the board that kept the public informed of the progress of the campaign. As the collection grew, the number of tanks increased to show how many tanks the collection would make. To get the community to the Victory Scrap Yard, there was entertainment every night. There was a stage, and the loudspeakers were set up so that the event could also be heard by anyone passing by on the street. To get into the show, you had to make a contribution to the salvage drive.[92] Imagine sitting in the scrap yard for an evening of entertainment, feeling a sense of pride and being surrounded by friends and neighbors who were all united for the war effort.

The campaign was a success. The scrap metal was purchased by scrap dealers who prepared it for industrial use. Lukens Steel Company purchased the iron and steel scrap from the scrap dealers, and paper was sold to paper mills in the area. The total weight of the salvage collected was 680,761 pounds.[93] The need for scrap to support the war effort drove the campaign, but the spirit of the community led to its success.

Salvage around Chester County

John Kathman, who lived in Phoenixville as a child during the war, described his personal memories of scrap drives during an interview with the author. He remembered collecting scrap as a child. There were two garages behind the house of one of his friends. He and his friends blocked off the space so that they could store the scrap they collected there. They made a "Scrap Yard" sign for the space, and they would go with their wagons and knock on doors around the neighborhood to see if people wanted to donate scrap. They received donations like pots and pans for the cause. He recalled that a truck would come to pick up the scrap at times.

In the November 2, 1943 issue of the *Daily Local News*, an advertisement, approved by the War Production Board, showed bombers smashing Nazi war plants with the caption "Vital Airplane Parts Are Being Made from Salvaged Waste Paper." Giving new meaning to recycling, the advertisement asked people to save "wrapping paper, store bags, boxes, cartons, corrugated paper and old newspapers" to overcome shortages. The advertisement also provided the names of local dealers that one could contact—"Downingtown Paper Co., S. Austin Bicking Paper Co. and Davey Company Downingtown, PA."

In West Chester, the unused railway tracks were removed as part of the scrap metal drive.

Even the U.S. Department of Agriculture got involved. It published a pamphlet, *Salvage for Victory*, which included details about collecting salvage around the farm. Since Chester County had many farms, this pamphlet was

Scrap collection at Chester County Courthouse, West Chester, Pennsylvania, 1942. *Photo by Jimmy John. Chester County Historical Society, West Chester, PA.*

Removal of the West Chester Street Railway rails for the scrap drive in West Chester, Pennsylvania, 1942. *Photo by Jimmy John. Chester County Historical Society, West Chester, PA.*

a valuable resource for farmers in the area. The pamphlet included a list of things to collect and provided instructions on how to organize and dispose of salvaged items.[94] It listed things around the farm to donate:

1. All kinds of scrap metal could be donated—old milk buckets, old tools, barbed wire or other metal items.
2. Bags and rags were other collectible items that could be donated, including old clothing and feed bags. These items could be used for other purposes. For example, old clothing and feed bags could be used as cleaning rags in factories.
3. Old rubber items like worn-out tires and overshoes could be used to make new tires.
4. Farmers were also reminded about the need for paper, and they were encouraged to save all types of paper, including cardboard boxes and newspapers. Salvaged paper was used to make paperboard for packing items like food and parts for military equipment.

Along with suggestions for collecting the salvage items, the pamphlet provided information on disposing of the items. Numerous options were provided: sell the salvage items to a "junk man," give it to "charities, schools, or other organizations" or take the items to a local dealer.[95]

There were also salvage posters used to encourage citizens to salvage vital material, like the "Save Every Ounce of Waste Paper" flyer from the Radnor Township Citizens Service Corps Salvage Committee. The flyer emphasized the importance of the salvage drive with the stunning statistic that waste paper was used by the army and navy to wrap or make 700,000 items.[96] Radnor Township is located just over the border of Chester County in Delaware County.

Throughout the county, efforts were made to support the war as individuals and communities adjusted their everyday lives to become a part of the mobilization effort.

A Radnor Township Citizens Service Corps Salvage Committee ad. *Courtesy of Tredyffrin Easttown Historical Society, Berwyn, PA.*

6

Preparing and Protecting the Homefront

The air and sea surveillance and missile defense system of the twenty-first century did not exist in 1940. There was no internet or twenty-four-hour news cycle with up-to-the-minute information on Hitler's blitz into Poland or images on the Internet of the displaced children during the Battle of Britain. People followed news reports of the war in the newspapers, watched newsreels before feature films at local theaters or listened to the radio, for those who had access to one. What was happening in Europe and Asia was a world away, and it probably seemed unlikely that an enemy so far from the United States posed a threat to the homeland. As the war escalated in Europe, civil defense became more important, and President Roosevelt recognized the need to build up the nation's home civil defense system. In 1940, the Council of National Defense was reestablished by the president. By1941, the Office of Civilian Defense (OCD) had been established to assist in the coordination of the nation's civil defense system.[97] There was not a lot of public enthusiasm for the OCD initially, but when Pearl Harbor was bombed on December 7, 1941, that changed. People were frightened by the possibility of an attack on the continental United States, and those who were not in the military were anxious to support the war effort in other ways. Many joined local civil defense organizations.

There were a variety of opportunities if you were interested in becoming part of the local civil defense program—auxiliary firemen, auxiliary police, air patrol workers, chaplains and medical corps were some of the options available. If you were a member of a civil defense

Cover of *The United States Citizens Defense Corps* publication. *From the collection of John A. Viglione.*

organization, you wore an armband or helmet with the OCD symbol when on duty. The symbol was a white triangle inside a blue circle. There was another symbol inside the white triangle to identify the specialty. For example, the medical corps' symbol was different than the air patrol workers' symbol.[98]

AIR RAIDS

Air raid protection was part of the civil defense program. The government published booklets with instructions on what to do during an air raid, and local newspapers also published information to instruct citizens on air raid procedures. Although the possibility of an enemy attack on the East Coast seemed remote, preparedness was a point of action.

Chester County was divided into zones, and Judge Butler Windle was named the chief warden. The Tredyffrin Easttown area was part of zone 3, which included "the Eastern Section of the County west to Coatesville." And volunteers in the area were trained and participated in blackout drills. In February 1942, a drill was conducted from 10:30 to 10:45 p.m. The air raid volunteers reported that the drill was a success and that all but 1 of the 587 homes that were in the designated blackout zone followed instructions.[99] The symbol for air raid wardens that was visible on their helmets and armbands was a red- and white-striped triangle inside a blue circle.

The defense corps also included airplane spotters who watched for enemy planes from designated locations. As a spotter in West Chester, you would watch for aircraft from the top of the Farmers & Mechanics Building, a well-known landmark in the city. The Tredyffrin Easttown area also had volunteers who were positioned on the rooftops. They had 168 volunteer observers plus 31 people on the emergency list in 1942. Initially, the lookout point was the roof of the junior high school, but it was later changed to the

Tredyffrin Township Building. Spotters were often sitting in a space that was open to the elements with no protection from bad weather. As an observer in the Tredyffrin Easttown area, the shift was only two hours, and a glass enclosed shelter was installed to help protect volunteers from the elements.[100] In Downingtown, there was a plane-spotting tower at the McIlvaine Farm near the intersection of Whitford Road and Route 30 in Exton.[101]

During an interview with the author, Margaret B. Chalfant, who lived in West Chester, recalled that when the whistle blew for an air raid drill, she lowered the blinds, pulled the curtains and, since her home had shutters, closed then, so no light escaped. She was a member of the Red Cross, and as a Red Cross volunteer, she had to report to the Red Cross building that was across from the courthouse until the all clear was given. Her husband was a dentist, and as medical personnel, he had to report to the west end of town in the event that his services were necessary. She also explained that anyone who was driving during a drill had to stop and turn their headlights off until the air raid was lifted. Chalfant

Mr. Woodward and Miss Miles watch for enemy aircraft from the top of the F&M Building, West Chester, Pennsylvania, 1942. *Photo by Jimmy John. Chester County Historical Society, West Chester, PA.*

described a "desperate feeling" about the possibility that a bomb would be dropped on West Chester. She thought there was more concern that a plane targeting the Valley Forge General Hospital in Phoenixville may stray off course and hit West Chester than that the enemy was targeting West Chester.

North of West Chester in Phoenixville, John Kathman wrote in an e-mail to the author that he recalled the blackouts during the war. His father made a blackout room in the basement; it had blackout curtains on the windows so they could put on a light and listen to the radio when they were in the room. He also had a neighbor who was an air raid warden, and he recalled that his neighbor would knock on the door of a home when he saw a light. He felt the drills were more psychological since the Germans probably did not have the capability to fly that far at that time.

Preparing and Planning for an Emergency

For people who were not interested in volunteering as part of the air raid group, there were other opportunities available. Volunteer options included becoming a driver, joining a rescue squad or becoming a member of the medical corps, to name a few. Even the Boy Scouts were part of the effort, as the scouts and leaders in the area enrolled in first aid classes connected with civil defense and the Red Cross.[102]

American Red Cross

As the United States entered the Second World War, the Red Cross rallied volunteers who wanted to support the mobilization efforts. Chester County was part of the Southeastern Pennsylvania Chapter of the Red Cross during the war. This chapter included Montgomery, Chester, Bucks, Philadelphia and Delaware—excluding Nether Providence Township—Counties. The chapter had more than ninety-four thousand volunteers during the war.[103] Red Cross stories from around Chester County demonstrate how the organization impacted the lives of local residents.

West Chester

Margaret B. Chalfant, who lived in West Chester during the war, was a Red Cross volunteer. She was taking a medical course at the Red Cross when she became interested in the organization and decided to join the Motor Corps. She said that there were twenty-six to thirty people in her group, and her training included a course on cars. She remembered that she knew most of the topics covered in that particular course. She grew up on a farm and learned to drive when she was twelve years old. Therefore, she was familiar with automobiles. She completed her training and became a member of the Motor Corps. She had a winter and summer uniform, and her work in the corps required her to be on-call day or night. When she was on duty, she would drive to the Red Cross location in town for her assignment. She usually picked up one of the two or three Red Cross vehicles that were available for driving to and from an assignment. She also had some assignments in Philadelphia that required her to take the train into the city. In those cases, she would walk from the train station in Philadelphia to the location of her assignment. She spoke of many experiences during her time with the corps. One of the more challenging experiences that she recalled was an assignment she had in Philadelphia. Two people usually went on assignments into the city, but she did not have a partner with her that particular day. When she arrived at her destination in the city, she was told that she would be transporting food to Hog Island near Philadelphia. The food was loaded in a large truck that was parked on the second level. Since she was not comfortable driving the truck from the second story of the garage, the people working at that location brought the truck to street level for her. The adventure continued as she found out that the truck had at least six gears that she did not know how to shift. Since there were no other drivers available, she did what she had to do—deliver the food. She drove the truck in low gear the entire way and successfully transported the food to the designated location. The story did not end there, since she still had to drive the truck back to its original location. Someone at the Hog Island center showed her how to shift gears for her return trip, and she drove the truck back to the Red Cross location without incident.

An experience she recalled that was especially touching involved a patient at the general hospital who was blind. She was driving him from the Valley Forge General Hospital to the navy yard in South Philadelphia. As they were traveling to the city, he told her that he had a new baby that he had never seen. He then said, "I'll never see the baby." She was especially touched when

Right: Margaret B. Chalfant's Motor Corps ID photograph, 1941. *Used with permission of the Chalfant Collection.*

Below: 1946 share certificate for the Red Cross fund. *Used with permission of the Chalfant Collection.*

FIVE DOLLARS PER SHARE

5 5

My SHARE in the

1946

RED CROSS

FUND

This is to Certify that H. L. Chalfant
NAME OF SUBSCRIBER

has subscribed to ___ Shares in the 1946 Red Cross Fund in support of the world wide work of the Red Cross in relief of suffering and want.

SOLICITOR'S SIGNATURE

CHAIRMAN 1946 FUND

he asked if he could feel her face. She consented, and he said that he "drew a picture of her face in his mind." One of the rules of the organization was that they were not allowed to ask patients questions, so she did not know his final destination or how his journey ended. She was active in the Red Cross for about ten years.[104]

Phoenixville

The Red Cross was also active in the town of Phoenixville, and people who lived in the Phoenixville area who were interested in volunteering to support the war effort found a range of opportunities available at the Red Cross. An article, "Red Cross Plays Large Part in Providing Aid: Organized Here in 1917," in the July 2, 1949 issue of the *Daily Republican* described the history of the Red Cross in the Phoenixville area. The article included Red Cross programs during World War II, some of which are highlighted below.

Canteen

Part of the training for canteen workers was learning how to prepare emergency meals. In 1942, after volunteers completed the Red Cross canteen course, several of them prepared and served snacks to blood donors at the Jewish Community Center. In August 1942, uniformed workers began going to the Reading Station to give each man who was leaving for the armed services a package with candy, cigarettes and gum. This was an effort, since the new recruits left at 6:00 a.m. They also served at birthday parties, dances and other special events at the Valley Forge General Hospital.

Sewing

The sewing program focused on many projects, including repairing used clothing, sewing new garments and making curtains for local hospitals. Members of the program also made and delivered garments to the Valley Forge General Hospital. In 1944, the sewing group sewed for 1,892 hours.

Motor Corps

The Motor Corps provided transportation for blood donors, canteen workers and patients going to and from other institutions. Volunteers were also responsible for pickup and delivery of things made by volunteers in the sewing program.

Flowers

There were even opportunities for those interested in flowers. In February 1944, two volunteers offered to buy flowers and arrange them at the Valley

Forge General Hospital two days a week. The program caught on, and regular deliveries of flowers where made to the hospital.

Paoli, Berwyn and the Tredyffrin-Easttown Townships Area

Similar to Phoenixville, there was a wide range of volunteer opportunities available to interested parties at the Paoli Branch of the American Red Cross.

Rescue Squads

The Rescue Squad of the Paoli Branch of the American Red Cross had eight men and one leader. They had three units—Berwyn, Paoli and Malvern. "Gas masks, helmets, picks, shovels, crowbars and a trailer" were part of the designated equipment for the squads.

Courses

If you were interested in home nursing courses and lived near Berwyn, a course sponsored by the Red Cross was offered at the Tredyffrin-Easttown High School in Berwyn. A motor mechanics course was offered at the Matthew's garage in Paoli.[105]

Sewing

The sewing and knitting group met to sew various items. Over three thousand items were sewn by volunteers in 1942.

Canteen

The canteen workers served lunch every day to the workers at headquarters. Canteen workers also prepared parties for servicemen. The volunteers were trained to use a mobile canteen. A mobile canteen could be used to feed large groups in case there was an emergency or a disaster.

Surgical Dressings

In 1942, the 390 volunteers from the Paoli Branch of the American Red Cross made sixty-eight thousand surgical dressings—sixty thousand for the armed forces and eight thousand for local emergencies.

Hospital Service

The branch's Gray Ladies worked in local hospitals reading to patients and writing letters for them.[106]

The efforts of the Red Cross across the county demonstrated how everyone united for the cause.

7

Supporting the Troops

Around the country, organizations like the YMCA (Young Men's Christian Association) were doing their part to support the war effort. The Coatesville YMCA program was emblematic of the extraordinary efforts put forth by members of the local community to support the troops and their families during the war.

The YMCA was part of the Coatesville community in 1940. That sense of community was exemplified when the Second World War began and it, like many YMCAs in the United States, mobilized to support members who were serving both at home and abroad. The Coatesville YMCA executive secretary, J. Irvie Hoffman Sr., felt the need to provide some form of support to the members of the Coatesville YMCA who were serving in the military. Hoffman was a "front-line YMCA worker during World War I." From that experience, he remembered how important letters from home were to those serving, and he decided to make that part of the organization's program during World War II. Sending a regular letter to those in the military became the cornerstone of the Coatesville YMCA program that reached beyond the Coatesville YMCA community to thousands of Chester County residents serving.[107]

The program began simply enough. Hoffman received the names of those entering the service from local draft boards, families and friends. Once a name and address were received, the person was automatically enrolled in the program and put on the mailing list. If you were on the list, you received a service notebook and a toiletry kit. The kits included items like a comb, toothpaste, shaving cream, soap, a bath towel, paper and a pencil.[108] Everyone enrolled in the program was also sent a letter written by Hoffman on a regular basis. As Christmas approached, there was a push to do something special for the holiday, so the program expanded to include a treat from home, the ever resilient fruitcake. The program was a resounding success, and at one point, as many as twelve thousand people reportedly received the publication.[109] Hoffman was very engaged in the program. He made personal appearances at local events, wrote thank-you letters to members in the community for their continued support and sent other correspondence to parents and donors. He also went to the train station to see new recruits off and visited the family of those killed or missing in action.

Newsletter

Hoffman initially hoped to send a letter from home every week to those who served. However, the reality of preparing the letter and paying the postage costs to mail the letter prohibited weekly mailings, so instead, letters were sent every three weeks. By 1943, the letters were more like a newsletter format. The multi-paged publication was called the *Coatesville Red Triangle*. The name came from the organization's logo at the time, which was a red triangle. The logo dated back to the late 1800s when a red triangle was proposed as the YMCA symbol.[110] The letter was like a piece of home for those serving far away from family and friends. The following is a glimpse into the lives of those serving and the community that supported them.

The Coatesville Red Triangle
November 1,

The Coatesville YMCA *Red Triangle* newsletter logo. *Used with permission from the General Archival Collection of the Downingtown Area Historical Society Downingtown, PA.*

Sports

Sports was a popular section in the newsletter. As a soldier during World War II, you did not have the luxury of television or the Internet to check the score of the local high school football team or to see if the Phillies had a chance at the World Series. Instead, news like that typically came from newspapers or letters from home. The newsletter included scores from local and professional games, and for some events, Hoffman provided play-by-play descriptions, capturing the excitement of the competition. Hoffman's response to a request for an update on Coatesville football went beyond the score as he described the game. "At last it happened. Under the impetus of a whirlwind third period attack that netted 2 touchdowns in 20 plays, Coatesville High won the Chester County title for the first time in 21 years, defeating Phoenixville 12–0 before 5,000 frosted spectators." Hoffman continued with game details and then went on to describe the fourth quarter. He said, "In the fourth quarter when Coatesville fumbled, Phoenixville struck with frustrated fury and advanced 24 yards to the 2 yard line. In fact, it was Coatesville's linemen who set the pace all afternoon."[111] Hoffman's descriptions were vivid and exciting. Readers also found sports updates that went beyond local sports, as Hoffman wrote about professional sports, too. The May 4, 1944 issue shared scores: "A's beat Yanks 8–4 and Phil's beat Giants in 12th 4–3 and snap five game winning streak." And that same year in September, Philadelphia baseball fans read the sad news as Hoffman wrote, "The Phil's are just playing so-so ball and there is no fight in the Natil. League except for 2nd place."

News from Home

From the homefront, Hoffman shared genuine, heartfelt stories. He told of his trip to the launching of a destroyer escort named the USS *George A. Johnson*. George A. Johnson was the first Lukens employee and Coatesville resident who was killed in action in 1942. "It was a beautiful sight to see the boat gracefully slide down the waves into the water," he wrote. There were also stories about visits he received from those on leave or returning home from the service. A sergeant stopped in to see Hoffman after just returning from the South Pacific. During the visit, he went into the movie theater, which was in the auditorium, and much to his surprise, the clip that was playing was of his own planes in action on Cape Gloucester. That had been his last mission before he came home.[112]

Letters from Those Serving

Letters arrived from men and women of varying ranks and ages. The letters were from all over the world and represented different branches of the military. Portions of letters that were received by Hoffman were written into each newsletter—what better way to share information and keep in touch than to use the words of the men and women serving all around the world? In the July 7, 1943 issue, letters were received from North Africa and the South Pacific to Camp Davis in North Carolina. There were bites about exotic places—hearing drum beats from native villages and seeing the sights of many Bible stories. There was a variety of correspondence that filled each issue. In May 1944, letters were written from battlefronts around the world, including foxholes in Italy, ships in the Pacific and battles in the Marshall Islands. Philip wrote, "I'm here in the Pac. and the going is tough at times, but we can take it. Just received three issues of the R.T. You'll never know how much it is enjoyed." Some wrote about unexpectedly meeting a friend or acquaintance from home even though they were a world away from Chester County. Private J. wrote from the Pacific, "Another Phoenixville boy, saw me sunning myself on the beach he stopped his truck so fast that I thought he put it in reverse. It's a small world after all."[113] The September 1944 issue included a section on nurses who were serving. The first paragraph was dedicated to them and included portions of letters from nurses in various locations, including France and Hawaii. Topics ranged from wounded soldiers from Normandy to how much the *Red Triangle* was enjoyed.

Events

Big events during the war were part of the newsletter. In the June 15, 1944 newsletter, Hoffman wrote, "D-Day is here? The big invasion is on and what a day to start writing the Triangle. Churches are all open and prayers are being said everywhere. In the church next door, down the street, on the Avenue and in all the homes." He wrote that on D-Day, there was an event going on at the YMCA, and he asked a local reverend to say a prayer "for the success of the invasion and for all you boys everywhere."

The May 23, 1945 issue began, "V-E Day longed for, prayed for, fought for, has come and gone prayerfully, soberly and seriously." The significance of the day was evident in some of the letters posted in that issue. Private George wrote, "I'm in the 4th Armored Div. of Genl. Patton's 3rd Army and what a rugged outfit. Seems like we no sooner take a town than we're on our way again." And Gladys from England wrote, "Have gotten in some released POWs. They are in pitiful condition."

Humor

Humor was a welcomed relief from the seriousness of the life and death situations that surrounded many in the armed services. Jokes and humorous stories told by Hoffman or written in letters from those serving were interspersed throughout the newsletter.

On December 12, 1942, Hoffman wrote that Corporal P.E. said he caught two mosquitoes "turning over his dog tag" to determine his blood type.

From the Middle East, Robert wrote, "More and bigger grasshoppers here than I've ever seen in my life. They look like small pursuit planes. Sometimes they get so bad in our tent we have to move our beds outside—the grasshoppers just take over."[114]

Hoffman also scattered humor throughout the issues—"Waitress: 'The man over there says his soup isn't 'fit for a pig.' Harassed Manager: 'Then for goodness sake take it away and bring him some that is.'"[115] In the February 10, 1944 issue, he wrote, "I heard this story: I went into a restaurant and hung up my coat. I put a sign on it. 'This coat belongs to a champion fighter—I'll be back.' So what? When I went to get my coat it was gone and there was a note that said: 'Taken by a champion sprinter and I won't be back.'"

FRUITCAKE

Whether you liked fruitcake or not, receiving it was a treat from home. The January 1944 issue had an illustration of solders eating the cake with the caption "We ate the cake box, too!" and over the course of the war, many wrote about the fruitcake. Some wrote about sharing their cake with others. In February 1944, Dorothy from N.A. wrote, "Thanks for the fruitcake. We all had a bite." And in May 1944, Tony wrote, "I just received a 'Fortress' full of Red Triangles and the long awaited fruitcake. They must have smelt the f.c. coming. By the time I reached my tent the whole squadron was in a line for the fruitcake chow."[116] On February 19,

The Coatesville YMCA initiated a fruitcake program, which coordinated sending ten thousand cakes to servicemen all over the world during World War II, 1943. *Courtesy of the YMCA of Greater Brandywine.*

1944, Hoffman wrote that 8,600 fruitcakes were sent and that they were still looking for a few addresses so that the remainder of the cakes could be delivered.

One man found the box his fruitcake was delivered in fifty years later and donated it to the YMCA. Here is the story the YMCA of Greater Brandywine shared about the donation:

> *This fruit cake box was returned to the Brandywine Y, in 1995 by Albert Belmont, who found it in his foot locker 50 years after returning from serving in World War II. Albert shared that during the war, he and his buddies were holed up in a wet, dark place in the jungles of the Pacific when mail arrived, including a fruit cake from the YMCA in Coatesville. Albert shared the cake with his fellow soldiers, who were jubilant to taste the little piece of home. Albert explained that the box contain*[ed] *more than just fruitcake—hope was woven through every bite. Albert added the fruit cake box to the Y archives so that future generations could remember the men who fought for our freedom and the Y that remembered the men.*[117]

After the War

The end of the war did not mean the end of the program, and in January 1946, nearly seven thousand *Red Triangles* were sent to those still in the service. There were also programs and events for those returning from military service. In the March 25, 1946 issue, there was a section that included a list of events for servicemen. There were many different activities that would appeal to varying interests. Sporting events included an ex-servicemen's basketball tournament, the Army–Navy football game in September in Coatesville and the Swimming Club. The Father & Son Club was holding an event at the end of March, and there were meetings of the Fruitcake Eaters Association (FCEA). During one of the FCEA committee meetings, the possibility of forming Red Triangle Clubs in local communities was discussed. Many returning from the military became a part of the FCEA, and the first picnic in August 1946 in Maryland was well attended by members and their families. The FCEA met until about 1950.[118] The program cost the YMCA approximately $250,000 over four years. Most of the expenses were related to mailing and preparing the publication and the fruitcakes sent at Christmas time.[119]

Today

Today, the Brandywine YMCA, in Coatesville, is now part of the YMCA of Greater Brandywine. Although the location has changed, the spirit of the organization continues. The YMCA's mission is to put Christian principles into practice through programs that build healthy spirit, mind and body for all.[120]

8
Colleges and Universities

Colleges and universities were open for business as the country mobilized from coast to coast. In Chester County, Immaculate University, Lincoln University and West Chester University were not only operational, they rose to the challenge of adapting to the new realities of campus life with a nation at war.

Immaculata University

Immaculata University is located near Malvern in Immaculata, Pennsylvania. The school, known as Immaculata College in September 1941, was a Catholic institution for women. It was founded as Villa Maria College by the Sisters, Servants of the Immaculate Heart of Mary, in 1920 when it was granted a charter. It became the first Catholic college for women in the Philadelphia region. In 1929, the name was changed to Immaculata College, and in June 2002, the school became a university.[121] As the country mobilized after Pearl Harbor Day, the staff, faculty and students of the school adjusted to changes in campus life and participated in the mobilization effort to support the homefront.

The Immaculata College campus began to feel the effects of the war in 1939 when a student from Italy and one from Germany came to campus to complete their education due to the unrest in Europe. There were also two religious sisters from Belgium who commuted to campus and a Franciscan sister from New York who had to cancel her studies in Poland due to the war.[122] These new members of the campus community were not just headlines from a newspaper story about the war in Europe; they were peers and colleagues who had personal stories to tell and daily reminders of the unrest overseas. Even with these reminders, when the new academic year began in September 1941, the war, a world away, did not personally affect the daily lives of most of the enrolled students. After the bombing of Pearl Harbor, that changed.

Curriculum

Following the bombing of Pearl Harbor, the United States was in a state of war, and Immaculata College was positioned to do what it did best: provide an education to prepare students for the future. The war affected everyday life for everyone, and curriculum changes were made to meet the challenges the nation had to face. Defense was a part of the national dialogue, and so defense courses were added to the curriculum. All students were required to attend a defense course one hour each week. Among the defense courses offered were defense mathematics, first aid, Occupational Therapy, Mechanical Drawing and a pre-flight course. There was a cookie canteen class that prepared students for work in Red Cross canteens, and the school also offered night classes to men and women for the national defense program. In addition to the inclusion of defense courses in the curriculum, in 1943 the school became the first college to implement an "accelerated scholastic program." If you were enrolled in the program, graduation was earlier than expected. Early graduation meant graduates could enter the workforce or military sooner. The war was on everyone's mind, so when the college offered the accelerated program, many students enrolled. In March 1943, the school newspaper, *Immaculatan*, reported that 64 percent of the students were planning to take the summer classes associated with the program that year.[123]

Campus Community

Changes in the campus community went beyond curriculum modifications. In 1940, a Red Cross unit was established on campus, and the students had a cookie canteen for baking cookies to send to men in the armed services. Civil defense also became a part of campus life as the school held blood drives and air raid drills. The beacon on the dome, a focal point of the college, was extinguished for a period of time. There were war bond drives and a committee to sell defense stamps. Overall, the war bond drives at the college resulted in the collection of over $1,180,000 from students, parents and faculty.[124] For these efforts, the school was awarded the Distinguished Service Citation, and according to the Treasury Department, a hospital plane was named after the school for its participation in the program.[125]

In addition to bond buying to help finance the war, the school also had a committee to conserve materials that were necessary for the defense buildup. And rationing was not limited to home; it was a part of campus life as well. Students were required to use their ration books from home when they ate on campus. New shoes also became a casualty of war since leather shortages limited the number of new pairs of shoes that could be purchased per year. Students did not seem to let the shortages affect their enthusiasm as they found creative solutions to work around them. For example, the shortage of nylon didn't stop the students who decided to use leg makeup for "painted" stockings. Immaculatans also joined the armed services. In May 1945, there were thirty-six graduates on the honor roll, according to the *Immaculatan*.[126]

Prisoners of War

As the war continued, large numbers of prisoners of war (POWs) were being captured, and over 400,000 Axis prisoners were sent to camps around the United States.[127] Some of these POWs became part of the campus landscape. The superintendent of the farms at Immaculata College used German POWs to help at harvest time. One prisoner wrote a touching letter to the school after he returned to Germany, saying he felt at home at the college. The prisoner went on to say, "Your kindness that gave me vital energy in the midst of a hateful world, I shall never forget. For all you gave me, I'll probably never be able to give you anything in return; yet I ask God to repay you for me."[128]

Immaculata University Today

Today, Immaculata College has grown from a small, liberal arts, women's college to Immaculata University, offering undergraduate, master's and doctoral degree programs. As of October 2014, the university offers seventy-eight degree programs, as well as certifications in non-degree programs. "In addition to courses on campus, there are thirty-five cohort groups at the undergraduate, masters and doctoral levels, offering courses in education, nursing and business." There are 111 full-time faculty members, which include 21 Sisters, Servants of the Immaculate Heart of Mary. [129]

Immaculata students visit with navy "chefs." *Courtesy of Immaculata University Archives.*

Lincoln University

Lincoln University is located in Lincoln University, Pennsylvania in southern Chester County. The university, like Immaculata College, also achieved a first in Chester County. Immaculata College was the first Catholic college for women in the Philadelphia area, and Lincoln University was a pioneer in education, becoming the first institution to provide higher education for males who were of African descent.[130] The university began in 1854 as the Ashmun Institute, and it became the nation's first "degree granting Historically Black College and University."[131] When the United States entered the war in December 1941, the university adapted to the new normal of a nation at war. Since the university was exclusively for African American men at the time, the impact of the war for African American soldiers was also of high interest to the campus community.

Curriculum

In October 1940, before the United States entered World War II, a Civil Aeronautics Authority (CAA) program was started at Lincoln University to study aviation. Some European countries had civilian pilot training programs leading up to the war, and in 1939, President Roosevelt signed the Civilian Pilot Training Act. The act established civilian pilot training programs through educational institutions. The program trained more pilots, and it provided opportunities for minorities, including African Americans and women, to be trained as pilots. Although it is not clear whether the CAA course offered at Lincoln University at that time was part of the civilian pilot training program, the course did train pilots. According to the school newspaper, the *Lincolnian*, there were ten students enrolled in the course. The airfield to be used for the course was a CAA-approved field near Oxford, and there was a "flight contractor" who would be in charge of the instruction. A student who enrolled in the class also had two other instructors, one for a navigation course and another for a meteorology course. In January, students in the course took their final examinations in meteorology and navigation, and there were also plans for a second semester. Although it is not clear how long the flight course was offered, the significance of it was felt by at least one student when he received an appointment to the Tuskegee Army Flying School. S. Albert Black was leaving Lincoln to enter the Army Air Force Advance Flying School in Alabama. The Tuskegee Army Flying School was set up to train African Americans in flight. The school trained the country's first African American military pilots. Over one thousand pilots were trained at the flying school, and the Tuskegee Airmen became one of the most respected fighter groups in the war. In addition to the aviation course, when the United States entered the war after the bombing of Pearl Harbor, there were other curriculum changes at the university. New course offerings included War and Society and Public Finance. A Hale America program was also offered by the Physical Education department to get students in better physical condition.[132]

Campus Community

The university was quick to organize a campus civil defense system after the bombing of Pearl Harbor. In early 1942, air raid wardens and first-aid workers were organized around campus. As an air raid warden, you focused on keeping order in case there was a disaster. First-aid workers were to deal with treatment of injuries. The plans included the assignment of a civil defense warden and a first-aid provider for every dormitory on

Lincoln University campus photograph from the 1943 yearbook. *From Special Collections and Archives, Langston Hughes Memorial Library, Lincoln University, Lincoln University, PA.*

campus.[133] The campus community also recognized the importance of conservation and salvage of resources that were vital to support the military. The December 1942 issue of the *Lincolnian* described salvage efforts on campus, noting that there was an increase in salvage collection efforts in comparison to the previous twelve-month period. The school's overall goal was to collect the "1,000 tons necessary to build a destroyer." The campaign was embraced throughout the campus community and included the caretaker of the university's dump and the building/grounds department.[134]

Lincoln University was an all-male school at the time, and like most colleges and universities in the country, enrollment was declining as people joined the armed services. At the same time, there was a shortage of housing for defense workers. The administration at the university decided to offer on-campus housing to local workers. As a result, extra dormitory space was provided to defense workers as a solution to housing shortages in the area. The new faces on campus numbered 150 defense workers from a plant in Elmo, Pennsylvania. The workers traveled to and from the plant by bus.[135]

Serving in the Armed Services

As part of the Selective Service Act, age-eligible students had to register for the military. In October 1940, there was an article in the *Lincolnian* about the registration of Lincoln University students for military service. Registration was held at the gymnasium on campus. Officials from the Oxford school district were set up from 7:00 a.m. to 9:00 p.m., and 139 students were registered at that time.[136] During the war there were many who served in the armed services from the university, and the student paper provided staff and students with updates on their status. "The Boys in Camp" column posted letters from those in the armed forces. If you were interested in writing to someone serving, you could check "Have You Written?" for a list of the names and addresses of those serving. The June 5, 1943 *Lincolnian* reported that the Ladies Auxiliary of Lincoln University sent baskets to "our boys." The baskets were financed by donations from students and faculty. In 1943, 134 students had gone into the armed services.[137] The declining effect on enrollment continued throughout the war years.

African Americans in the Military

The status of African Americans in the war was an important issue to the student body. The *Lincolnian* kept students informed and engaged by publishing articles about this issue. Articles like "Negro Personnel in Army Totals over 450,000" provided details about those serving, which included the branches of the military they were serving in and locations of deployment.[138] The headline of another article in the same issue was "Committee for Mixed Army Announces Meeting: L.U. Student Chairman." According to the article, a senior at Lincoln University was elected chairman of a committee that was being organized for anyone interested in the "formation of an experimental mixed army unit." If you were interested, the next meeting date and a list of the other members of the committee were posted.

The December 14, 1943 issue of the Lincolnian reported the success of the NAACP (National Association for the Advancement of Colored People) student conference. According to the article, 177 delegates attended the "Fifth Annual N.A.A.C.P. Student Conference on October 29–31 on Lincoln's campus." Job discrimination, voting and "equalization of teachers' salaries" were just a few of the topics discussed.[139]

In 1944, the university sponsored a guest speaker on campus, Ollie Steward. Steward was a correspondent from the Afro-American Newspapers. He described his journey to different parts of the world, his experiences with people he met and his observations of "Negro soldiers on the battle front." He traveled around the world, including New York, Europe, Iran, Iraq and Africa. He had the opportunity to meet President Roosevelt and Winston Churchill. One of the main purposes of his trip was to observe African American soldiers in the battle zones to get a sense of their living conditions and equipment. He also had the opportunity to sample opinions of those serving. He shared with the audience that he found the soldiers were "able and capable under enemy fire" and that living conditions were the same as their white counterparts. They had the best equipment, and although reactions and opinions varied, the basic trend was that there would be a better life in the postwar world.[140]

Lincoln University Today

Lincoln University is located in southern Chester County. The university offers undergraduate programs in the arts and sciences, as well as a variety of graduate programs. Lincoln University has satellite campuses in Philadelphia and Coatesville. The university's current enrollment is approximately two thousand students.[141]

West Chester University

The origin of West Chester University dates back to the early 1800s, when a group established the West Chester Academy. The school evolved over the years, and in 1927, when Pennsylvania introduced a four-year teacher education program, the school became West Chester State Teacher's College. During the Second World War, West Chester State Teacher's College took up the challenges the homefront faced.[142] Those who remained home did their best to support the effort as life on campus was transformed by the war.

Campus Community

Even before the bombing of Pearl Harbor, students at the college were being touched by the war overseas. In April 1941 came the sad news of the plane crash off the coast of Virginia that resulted in the death of the first casualty from the college, George Nelson Blackburn.[143] And in June, nine men who were enrolled in a CAA course finished the class. In December, when the United States declared war, life on the campus of the college took a dramatic shift as the college wasted no time taking on the challenges faced by the country. A week after the bombing of Pearl Harbor, the college had a practice air raid, and a chief air raid warden was appointed. Civil defense and air raid drills became part of the routine on campus as student squadrons were organized in areas like first aid and rescue. A siren was installed on Old Main,[144] and plans to purchase green window blinds for every room or opening in the dormitory were made in the case of an emergency at the July 1942 board meeting.[145] The student body continued to enjoy night football games during the 1942–43 school year, but there were specific air raid instructions to be followed. As male students left for the armed services, enrollment declined, which also had an effect on extracurricular activities, such as male athletic teams.[146]

Students felt the effects of the programs and campaigns that were part of the mobilization effort at home and at school. Bond sales were not only part of life at home but were also promoted on campus to both students and faculty members to help finance the war. The employees of the school showed their support for the effort in 1943 when 100 percent participated in the governor's campaign for state employees to purchase defense bonds and stamps. Rationing also became a part of campus life, and students had to bring in their ration books when they ate twelve or more meals at school. Collecting scrap was part of the homefront effort, and during the 1942–43 academic year, the school's scrap collection efforts had a unique twist. There were two cannons on Wayne Field. The thought was to donate the cannons to the town's scrap efforts, but first the donation had to be cleared with the necessary authorities. Since no historical significance was identified for the cannons, the donation was cleared. The plan was to take the cannons to the collection center in West Chester. Showing the enthusiasm of the campus community to support the effort, students, accompanied by the band and faculty, marched in a parade to the collection site on West Market Street.[147]

A student group discusses war at the Intercollegiate Conference on Government and World Affairs, West Chester State Teachers College, 1941–42. *Courtesy of Photograph Collection, Special Collections & Archives, West Chester University Library, West Chester, PA.*

Students listening to war news, West Chester State Teachers College,1941–42. *Courtesy of Photograph Collection, Special Collections & Archives, West Chester University Library, West Chester, PA.*

Curriculum

The college, like Immaculata College and Lincoln University, also instituted changes in the curriculum. Courses such as Climatology, Meteorology and Home Nursing were a few of the classes added to the college's course schedule. In addition, the school introduced the "long summer" program, which was a proposal to speed up the teacher training program.[148]

United States Postal Unit

The president of the school worked on a plan to have a United States Postal Unit for military postal students set up on the college campus. In February 1943, the board passed a motion to approve the plan for the college to enter into a contract with the United States Army. The contract allowed the army to use certain college buildings and equipment for the postal unit. The first group of men arrived March 1943. They remained on campus until 1944, when the government notified the school that they planned to end the contract for the Army Postal School.[149]

Newspaper

Like any college newspaper, the school's paper, *Quad Angles*, was a great resource for the students and staff. In September 1943, changes came to the newspaper. The size was reduced from seven to five columns. Soldier updates were posted in "V…__Mail," and "The Boys Write" section printed portions of letters from those serving. Copies of the *Quad Angles* were sent to those in the military. As the war came to an end in 1945, the number of stars on the school's service flag was one thousand, with twenty-three gold stars that represented those from the college community who sacrificed their lives during the war. "Peace Brings Changes to West Chester Campus" was the headline in the September 1945 issue of *Quad Angles*, and enrollment grew to around one thousand at that time. According to the paper, the college's rising enrollment included servicemen who were returning to campus to complete their studies. The college was looking forward to the future.[150]

West Chester University Today

West Chester University is the largest of the fourteen higher education institutions that make up the state's system of higher education. The university offers over one hundred graduate and undergraduate programs. West Chester University also offers distance education courses and programs at a location in Philadelphia.

9

Caring for the Troops

In preparation for the large numbers of casualties expected from the battlefield, the United States Army's Medical Department constructed military hospitals around the United States. There were over 670,000 wounded during World War II who received medical treatment in the combat zone as well as at mobile units and fixed hospitals overseas. Those wounded who still needed hospitalization were transferred to one of the military hospitals in the United States. Due to its proximity to Philadelphia and New York City, a farm in Charlestown Township in the northeastern part of the county, near Phoenixville, was selected as the site for one of these hospitals, the Valley Forge General Hospital.[151]

Surrounding Community

The decision to build a military hospital in Chester County near Phoenixville would impact the town and the surrounding communities, as the once tranquil farm site would be transformed into a busy medical complex. Phoenixville had a population of 12,282 according to the 1940 census. It was a small community, and there were industries like the steel mill and small businesses that provided services and jobs. Residents of the area must have felt some uncertainty about the impact the influx of patients, families and staff associated with the hospital would have on the community. But when the hospital opened, the community responded. John Kathman, who lived in Phoenixville as a child at the time of World War II, recalled during an interview with the author that the town was supportive of the war effort, saying, "Everybody was in the effort," and when the hospital center came, the "town grew." During the author's interview with Virginia C. Groff, who worked in the Civilian Personnel Department at the hospital at the time, she shared her impressions of the town. She recalled that Phoenixville was a "sleepy town" where you could meet every "race and religion." It was "like a little New York." She, too, recalled how everybody in the town "rallied around" the war effort. Community support even extended to some local residents opening their homes to those in need of housing. Living quarters for the civilians working at the center or for people visiting patients were not available on campus. As a result, there was a need for housing in the area. John Kathman recalled that his mother and other residents in town took boarders into their home to help meet the demand for housing. He spoke of a female boarder who stayed with his family while she worked with blind

THE FIRST CONVOY MAKES HISTORY

Valley Forge officially opened for business with the arrival of the initial hospital train from coast evacuation hospitals. Most of Phoenixville's residents turned out to greet the first arrivals.

The first patients arrive. *Historical Society of the Phoenixville Area, Phoenixville, PA.*

The chapel. *Historical Society of the Phoenixville Area, Phoenixville, PA.*

patients at the hospital. He also remembered that some of the soldiers would come to the church in town for services even though there was a chapel on the hospital campus. One particular Sunday, his mother invited two soldiers who were standing outside the church after services to their home for breakfast. The two soldiers accepted the invitation, and they "kept coming." They not only became friendly, but his mother introduced one of the soldiers to a cousin, and the soldier and his cousin eventually got married.[152]

A COMMUNITY UNTO ITSELF

Construction of the Valley Forge General Hospital began in May 1942. When the hospital opened in February 1943, there were ninety-eight brick buildings, as well as additional buildings that were necessary to service the hospital. In the hospital there were operating rooms, labs, dental offices and even mobile X-ray units that could be used for patients who were confined to bed. There were different specialties at the hospital. The staff included several hundred doctors and nurses; in

Valley Forge General Hospital administration building. *Chester County Historical Society, West Chester, PA.*

addition there were army personnel and administrators. Civil service employees were also added to the staff. Other facilities in the complex included a fire department and police department. There was also a Post Exchange (PX, a government subsidized store on a military base that sells goods to military and other authorized personnel), post office, bowling alley, theater, library, dining hall, gymnasium, golf course, chapel and barracks—including a barracks for prisoners of war. The complex was like a small community unto itself.[153]

MEDICAL SERVICES

The hospital cared for patients who were injured during the war specializing in areas like plastic surgery, psychiatry and working with the blind.[154] Many of the plastic surgery patients who were sent to Valley Forge General Hospital had injuries that caused severe disfigurements.[155] Virginia C. Groff, who worked in the civilian personnel department, stated during an interview with the author that she had to write job descriptions and determine salaries for different employees. She recalled a female employee who worked with the plastic surgeons at the hospital and referred the author to an article in *Main Line Today* about this employee's work. According to the *Main Line Today*

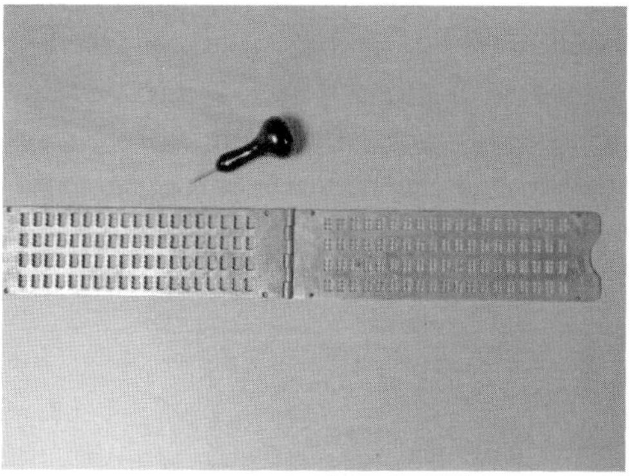

A braille slate and stylus. *Courtesy of John Kathman.*

article, this employee began working with patients with neuropsychiatric disorders teaching them how to paint. The surgeon in command at the hospital approached her and asked her to make masks of patient's faces to help surgeons with reconstructive surgery. She was to make masks of a patient's face before each surgery to help guide the surgeon. She made the masks using plaster of Paris.[156] In addition to facial reconstruction surgery, the hospital also worked with disfigured or missing limbs.

Rehabilitation of the blind was another area of specialization at the hospital. John Kathman remembered seeing staff from the hospital working with blind soldiers in town when he was a child. A patient, accompanied by a member of the hospital staff, would be dropped off at Fifth and Main Streets. The goal was for the patient to find the "way into town." During this time, his mother had a boarder who worked with the blind soldiers teaching them how to read braille. While she stayed with his family, she taught him how to read braille and even gave him a braille writer. He remembered using the device to write notes to soldiers. Kathman told a story that reflected the success of the program. In the 1950s, he lived next to a blind soldier who received treatment at the hospital. He described the neighbor as a "marvel," remembering how he cut his grass and waxed a car. The staff worked tirelessly to help the patients who had sacrificed so much for the country.

Community Life

Valley Forge General Hospital was like a community with a life of its own. Anyone who was a part of the hospital center had access to a chapel for religious services, a theater, the PX and recreational facilities. As an employee at the hospital, Virginia C. Groff recalled celebrities like Joan Crawford,

Helen Keller and the Duke and Duchess of Windsor visiting the hospital. Sports were also a part of the community life. There was a swimming pool, a golf course and a gymnasium, as well as basketball and bowling teams. Virginia C. Groff was a member of the women's basketball team and remembers that the women's team played teams from other industries. She also recalled that the men's team played other colleges and that they were invited to play at Madison Square Garden.

The Forge

Like in any community in the 1940s, there was a newspaper. The *Forge* kept everyone up to date on the events happening at the hospital center. It was published for the personnel of the general hospital in Phoenixville. The paper contained regular columns as well as articles about new patient programs or upcoming events at the hospital center. There was something for everyone in the *Forge*. Whether you were a patient or a member of the hospital staff, front-page headlines kept you up to date on events from entertainment on campus to news about the new pay schedule. "Hospital Post Theatre Nears Completion," "Blind Soldier Regains Sight: Awarded Congressional Medal," "VFGH Chief Nurse now Lt. Colonel" and "How GIs Vote" were just a few of the headlines on the front page of the July 29, 1944 issue.

Inside that issue was a story about the Gray Ladies, who were part of the American Red Cross.[157] They were helping with craft activities as part of the reconditioning program at the hospital. Thanks to the number of volunteers, the program was able to step up its schedule. The *Forge* also printed stories about the relationship between the hospital and the community. In December 1944, the Non-Commissioned Officers Club had a party for the Phoenixville children whose fathers were in the service. The party was held at the USO. The same month, the American Legion brought 2,500 gifts for the patients.[158]

News about celebrities, entertainment at the hospital center and movie schedules must have provided a welcome relief from the daily surgical and treatment schedules, whether you were a patient or a staff member. And of course, there was the sports section with information about professional sports as well as the Valley Forge General Hospital intramural sports teams. What better way to start the day than to read about the hospital's basketball team's twelve-game winning streak in December 1944?

In the July 29, 1944 issue, there was a compelling story told by Paul, who was at the hospital center for facial surgery. He recounted his experience on D-Day in Normandy. He recalled that they were briefed on the mission they were to follow before they were dropped behind enemy lines. Then the day for the mission came. He recounted, "That very minute we were starting on a mission that was to be the most important one of our lives...As our plane crossed the channel a large convoy of ships were spotted below. From this convoy the lead plane received orders to go ahead. This was the real thing." He went on to describe how the plane was hit by a barrage that shook the plane and the men were thrown to the floor. "The pilot managed to regain his altitude, and after a few minutes, another storm of gunfire greeted us. One motor was knocked out, but again the pilot pulled up, recovered his elevation and flew on." When they were over occupied France, the pilot gave the signal to jump. He jumped and landed in a tree in an orchard. He was one of two who made it to the designated rendezvous point. The two of them eventually met a group from other planes, and they began their mission, which was to demolish German supply lines. The goal was to prevent the Germans from receiving more supplies and support troops. He was injured by a piece of shrapnel that went through his cheek to the other side of his face. The group continued on until they reached a camp for the paratroopers. The story went on to describe the surgical treatment he was receiving at the hospital.[159]

PRISONERS OF WAR

Prisoners of war (POWs) were being captured in large numbers, and hundreds of thousands of Axis prisoners were sent to the United States and put in camps across the country. At the same time the prisoners were coming to camps in the United States, there were labor shortages throughout the nation, and using prisoners for laborers was being considered. Pennsylvania was one of the locations where prisoners were sent to help overcome labor shortages on farms and military posts, and Valley Forge General Hospital became one of the centers that housed POWs. In January 1945, the commanding officer of the hospital, Colonel Henry Beeuwkes, announced that prisoners of war were coming to the area to live in a fenced stockade at the hospital center. The prisoners

A plaque on the administration building of the University of Valley Forge, Phoenixville, Pennsylvania. *From collection of John Viglione.*

arrived on February 6, 1945. The commanding officer invited the press to an inspection by the "chief of staff of the Third Service District" of the prisoner's barracks a little over a week after they arrived.[160] The press was permitted to interview the commander in charge of the military police who guarded the prisoners. They also had the opportunity to talk to some of the POWs using interpreters. An article in the *Philadelphia Bulletin* on February 23, 1945, about the POWs at the Valley Forge General Hospital reported that the camp followed the Geneva Rules for treatment of prisoners, which included permission for prisoners to work. The Geneva Convention protocols stated that POWs could be put to work if they were paid.[161] The *Philadelphia Bulletin* article pointed out that "80-cents-a-day" was "payable only in coupons cashable at the canteen."[162] With fears that some prisoners might escape, the issue of security had to be addressed when considering the possibility of putting POWs to work. Eventually, many POWs went to work where minimum security was required. Virginia C. Groff remembered them cleaning her office. When not working, the prisoners enjoyed hobbies like playing the piano, carving wood chess pieces and playing chess or checkers. Their work at the Valley Forge General Hospital was usually as general laborers, bakers or electricians. The prisoners represented different branches of the German military, and they ran their own mess hall and PX. The end of the war did not mean that the prisoners were immediately sent home as many expected. In fact, the POWs at the Valley Forge General Hospital did not leave until June 1946.[163]

After the War

After World War II, the hospital continued to operate, providing care for the wounded from the Korean and Vietnam Wars until it closed in 1974. Today, the University of Valley Forge (formerly Valley Forge

Christian College) is located on a large portion of the site where the hospital was built. Many of the original buildings are used by the university, including the current administration building that once housed the offices of the commanding officer. The university embraces the history of the site and held a ceremony commemorating the Valley Forge General Hospital in 2012.

10
Stories from around Chester County

Alumni News

The Downingtown Area High School Alumni Association published a newsletter called *Alumni News* from August 1943 through November 1945. The newsletters, sent free to alumni in the armed services, were filled with news from home, updates on those serving in the military and letters from alumni serving around the world. The front-page headlines ranged from reunion news to tributes to alumni who were killed or missing in action. You could also find updates about bond sales around the area by checking the paper. Some issues of the paper included a chart that summarized bond sales by local towns. The "Our Town" section shared news about people and events at home. In the May 1944 issue, the photograph of West Lancaster Avenue in the "Our Town" column, along with the description of the forsythia blooming all over town, was like a breath of spring from Pennsylvania.[164] Those serving were the priority of the newsletter, and at the Fifty-seventh Alumni Banquet, the alumni who were serving in the armed forces were honored. The Honor Roll was placed in front of the hall during the banquet, and at the speaker's table there were representatives from the armed services. Representatives included a WAC (Women's Army Corps) and a WAVE.

Along with general updates about alumni in the military, the "Purple Ink" section printed soldiers' letters or sections of letters sent to the paper as they

Downingtown Jr./Sr. High School, 1940s. *Used with permission from the Photo Archives of the Downingtown Area Historical Society, Downingtown, PA.*

shared their experiences from all over the world. Those writing the letters described details of their travels to places like Egypt and Australia, and some shared their observations about different cultures. Many wrote about the *Alumni News*, expressing gratitude for the paper and praising the quality of the publication. The November 1, 1945 issue of the *Alumni News* was dedicated to those who served, with a special section that listed the names of the alumni who died during the war.

Boy Scouts

During the war, the Boy Scouts participated in various activities supporting the war effort. The scouts and scout leaders enrolled in first-aid classes with the Red Cross.[165] In an article in the *Daily Local News* on January 18, 1942, the Chester County Council of the Boy Scouts of America decided to cancel its annual meeting in response to the government requests to limit travel. In the same article, the scouts were given credit for participation in salvage of paper, metal and rubber during the year. And they distributed posters and other printed materials for the government and others. The Boy Scouts also experienced an unexpected consequence of the war. There was a shortage of manpower for leadership positions in the organization. Men who would typically take leadership positions in the Boy Scouts were in the military. Board members were urged to encourage men to join scouting.[166]

Bus Schedules

In May 1943, the Main Line Transfer Company initiated "War Emergency Schedule No. 1." The reduction in bus services was the direct result of a government requirement to reduce bus mileage as a gas-saving measure. The change affected the schedule, which included some towns in Chester County—West Chester, Malvern, Paoli and Berwyn.[167]

Celebrations

A victory parade was held on September 11, 1945, at 7:30 a.m. in Oxford. The parade included floats, displays and music. There were several bands that participated in the parade, including the Naval Band from Maryland and the Lukens Band from Coatesville.[168] The *Daily Local News* from September 12, 1945, reported a crowd of twenty thousand to twenty-five thousand attended the Oxford Victory Parade. "Oxford has Second Largest Parade in its History" was the headline in the *Oxford News* on September 13, 1945. The article described the event as one "of the outstanding events in a town noted for its wonderful parades."

Medical

The School of Nursing at the Chester County Hospital in West Chester participated in the U.S. Cadet Corps. The Cadet Corps was an accelerated training program for nurses. The government paid for the training of the nurses in exchange for military service. During World War II, over fifty graduates of the school served in the armed services.[169]

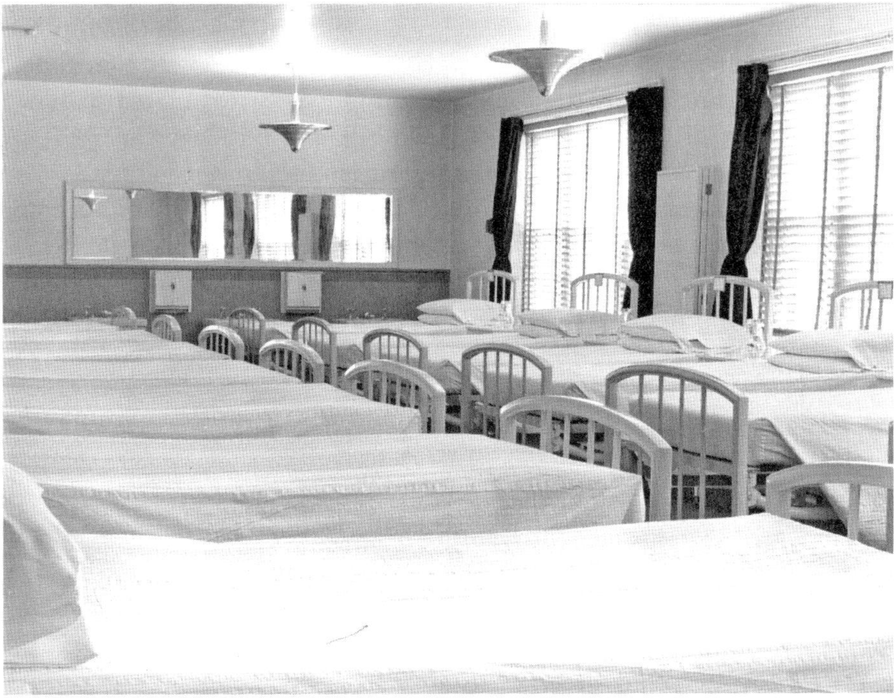

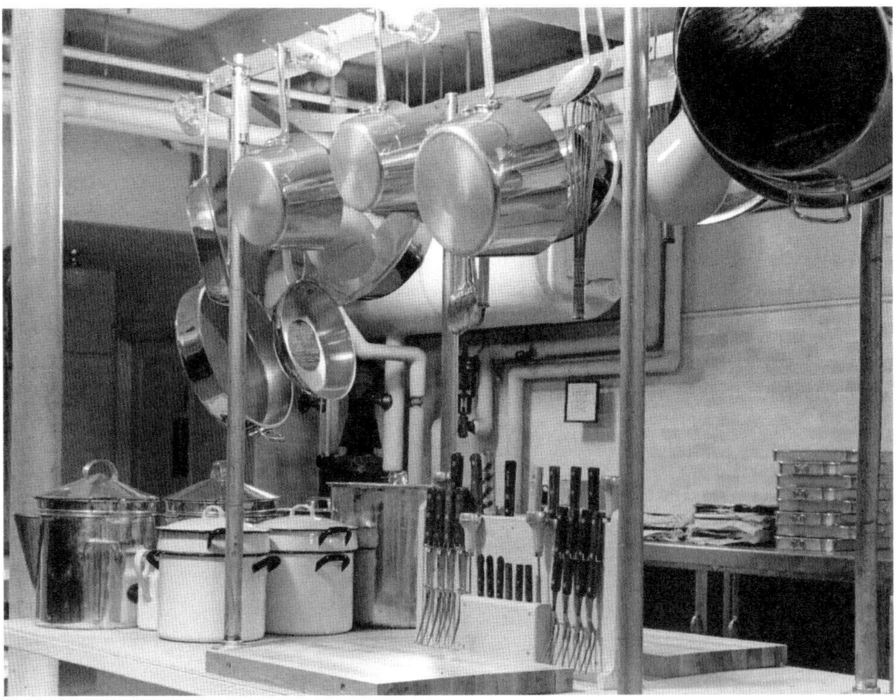

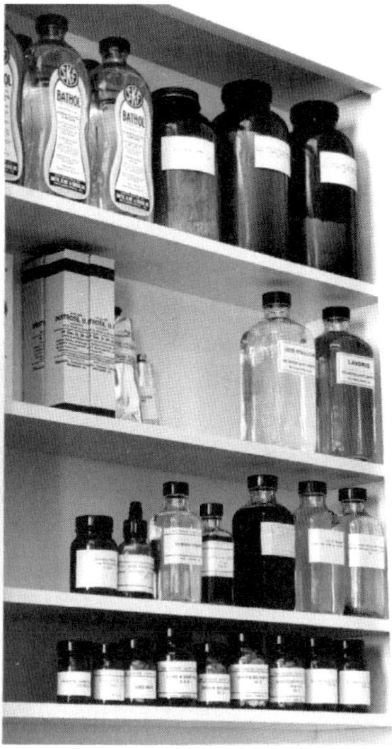

This page and opposite: "Emergency Hospital at Longwood": In May 1942 Mr. P.S. du Pont made an agreement with the Emergency Medical Service of the Chester County Council of Defense to equip and maintain an emergency hospital at the Longwood Conservatory, consisting of 42 hospital beds, 30 hospital cots and the necessary sheets, blankets, pillows, pillow cases and mattresses to service them. Also the necessary towels, wash cloths, trays, table ware, and kitchen utensils for a hospital of 72 patients. This emergency hospital was kept in readiness for any emergency for the agreed 2 year period. In September of 1944 Mr. du Pont asked the Hospital Committee of the Chester County Council of Defense to have the Longwood Conservatory property cleared of all hospital facilities, distributing the equipment to the various hospitals in Chester County and one in Newark, Delaware, and the property returned to its original status as of May, 1942. The bills for the hospital expenditures; supplies, equipment, & etc., for the installation of this emergency hospital amounted to $8,529. 72. *Text and image courtesy of Longwood Gardens.*

Military Accidents

The war touched close to home in Chester County on December 4, 1943, when a B-24 bomber crashed in West Nantmeal Township. The plane was on a routine training flight from Will Rogers Field in Oklahoma to the Reading Air Field. When it reached the Reading Air Field, it was unable to land due to poor visibility. The controller at the Reading Air Field reported in an affidavit that he provided the pilot with information on the weather conditions at nearby airports in Harrisburg and Philadelphia. He also reported that the last radio contact with the flight was at 10:54 p.m.[170] In another affidavit given by Sargent John S. Gillespie, a survivor of the crash, he recalled that the pilot was in communication with the Reading Air Field. They were unable to land in Reading, and the pilot informed the crew that they were going to land in Philadelphia. He also told the crew that their gasoline supply was low, and the crew was told to put on their parachutes. The plane crashed a short time later.[171] The plane wreckage was spread over a two-hundred-yard area on a farm in West Nantmeal Township. Two of the eleven crew members survived the crash. One of the survivors later died from his injuries. The remaining survivor, Sargent Gillespie, though seriously injured, recovered from his injuries.[172]

On May 7, 1944, a B-25 Mitchell Bomber crashed near the northern limits of the borough of West Chester. The plane was on a routine training

A memorial for crew on B-25 Bomber in Oaklands Cemetery, West Chester, Pennsylvania. *Photo by John A. Viglione.*

flight from Newark, New Jersey, to Kissimmee, Florida, when it crashed in the woods adjacent to the Oaklands Cemetery. Weather conditions were poor, and at the time of the crash, it was reported that rain and hail were falling. Residents reported that the plane "seemed to stop in midflight" before it nosed downward and began spinning. As it fell, its nose dove into the ground, and the plane exploded. The entire seven-man crew died in the accident. State police, firemen, ambulances and an army detail responded.[173] A memorial at the Oaklands Cemetery honoring the crew is a somber reminder of the dangers those who served faced even on the homefront.

MILKWEED

Japan's occupation of Java during the Second World War was of strategic importance to the United States. The plant fiber kapok used in life vests was imported from Java, and since Japan controlled the area, a substitute for kapok had to be found. The milkweed pod was such a resource. Milkweed floss was not only buoyant, it was also waterproof.[174] In 1944, the War Food Administration put out a call for the collection of milkweed to be used in lifejackets and other preservers to offset the shortage of kapok. The plan to harvest the milkweed encompassed twenty-one states, including Pennsylvania. As part of the collection plan, farmers were asked to allow milkweed to grow to maturity, instead of cutting it down, so that it could be harvested.[175] It was important for the pods to be collected at the right time, and bags for collecting the pods were provided by the government. The bags were distributed by local school officials.[176] Collectors were paid for the number of bags they collected.[177] Children in Chester County were mobilized as part of the collection efforts, and organizations like the Boy Scouts and the Girl Scouts participated. By September 23, according to a story in the paper, the superintendent of schools was "swamped" by the amount of milkweed floss received. The collection was so great that the principal of the Willistown Consolidated School reported that he was "about to be pushed out of his office" because of the pods and that the children in his school had responded "100 percent."[178]

RED CROSS

A sewing and knitting unit was set up in Honey Brook under the Coatesville Branch of the Red Cross. The unit's efforts went to refuge relief.[179]

SHORTAGES

On March 8, 1941, the *Daily Local News* article "War Defense Aided by Recapping Tires" emphasized the importance of conserving to help deal with shortages of vital resources like rubber. Drivers were encouraged to take care of tires and to have them recapped when needed.

SOLDIERS

Oxford hung a service flag on Third Street to honor those who were serving. The flag had 172 blue stars and 4 gold stars, according to the *Oxford Press*, November 25, 1942.

The Honey Brook Honor Roll was dedicated on December 11, 1943. The Honor Roll in front of Honey Brook High School included the names of about two hundred serving in the armed services, men and women.[180]

WAR BONDS

The September 16, 1943 issue of the *Daily Local News* reported that the Chester County chapter of the Daughters of the American Revolution reported $87,975 in war bonds purchased.

"Parkesburg Bond Drive is Over Top," was the headline in the *Coatesville Record* on October 2, 1943. Not only had the Parkesburg-Atglen area had a successful bond campaign, but the Parkesburg Air Raid groups also were organized at the local school.

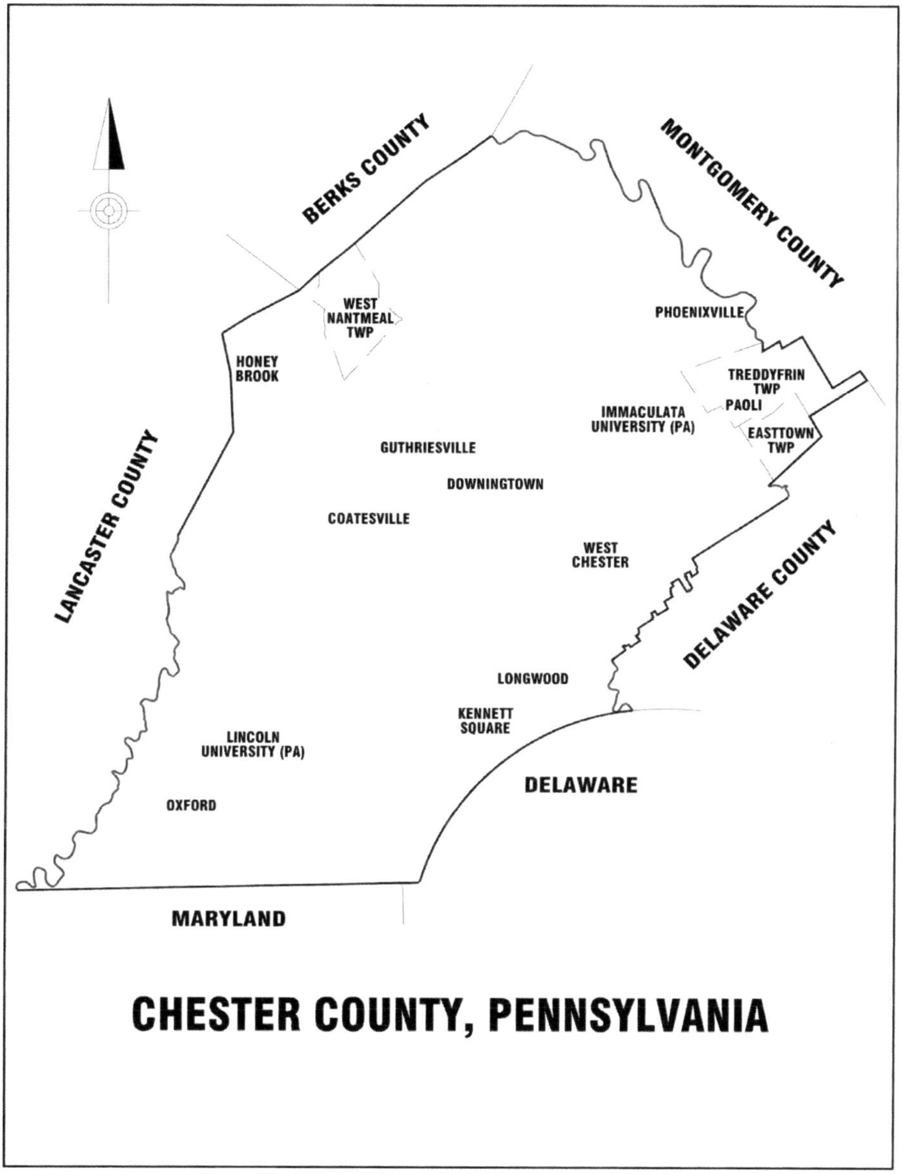

The map of Chester County highlights the different locations throughout the county mentioned in the book. The search for information about the Chester County homefront during World War II followed a path from one resource to the next all around the county. *Courtesy of Ronald A. Tajc.*

Notes

Chapter 1

1. ExplorePAHistory, "Stories from PA History."

Chapter 2

2. National WWII Museum, "Timeline."
3. U.S. Bureau of the Census, *No. 1430.*
4. Ibid., *Sixteenth Census of the United States.*
5. National WWII Museum, "Timeline."
6. Ibid., "Take a Closer Look at the Draft."
7. Ibid., "Timeline."
8. U.S. Bureau of the Census, *No.1430.*
9. History Place, "Franklin D. Roosevelt."
10. Klein, *Call to Arms.*

Chapter 3

11. Roosevelt, "104—Address at Shibe Park."
12. DiOrio, Gould Pella and Smith, *Remarkable Past*, 2–4.
13. Ibid., 2–8.
14. Martinez, "Paying Honor to a Woman of Steel."

15. ExplorePAHistory, "Arsenal of America."
16. DiOrio, Gould Pella and Smith, *Remarkable Past*, 17–8.
17. Sheehan, *Technology of World War II.*
18. In May 2014, the Steel & Iron Museum hosted a presentation about the USS *John W. Brown*. The speaker highlighted the company's contributions to the Liberty ship program during World War II. The speaker also stated that, during a recent maintenance check, it was discovered that some bottom plates had to be replaced on the ship. Luckily, bottom plates that were donated by Lukens Steel were found in storage and used for the repairs, allowing the ship to continue operating and providing Living History Cruises. Liberty Ship USS *John W. Brown* lecture, May 2014, https://www.youtube.com/watch?v=EbrK1ZRj9L4.
19. National WWII Museum, "WWII Veterans Statistics."
20. DiOrio, Gould Pella and Smith, *Remarkable Past*, 18.
21. History.com, "American Women in World War II."
22. *Lukens Plate*, January 21, 1944.
23. Ibid., February 6, 1942.
24. Ibid., September 4, 1942, 1.
25. Ibid., February 5, 1943.
26. Ibid., February 6, 1942.
27. Ibid., January 21, 1944.
28. Service flags were authorized by the Department of Defense to indicate the number of people serving from a family or organization. The blue star represented the number of those serving, and the gold star was for those who had sacrificed their lives.
29. DiOrio, Gould Pella and Smith, *Remarkable Past.*
30. National Iron & Steel Heritage Museum archives.
31. *Philadelphia Inquirer*, "Phoenix Iron & Steel Company."
32. Ibid.
33. Klein, *Call to Arms*, 136–40.
34. *Phoenixville (PA) Daily Republican*, May 21, 1941.
35. President Roosevelt made a series of radio broadcasts, beginning in 1933, to the American people on various topics that became known as fireside chats.
36. *Phoenixville (PA) Daily Republican*, June 2, 1941.
37. Ibid., May 25, 1942.
38. Klein, *Call to Arms*, 298.
39. *Phoenixville (PA) Daily Republican*, January 11, 1943.
40. Ibid., September 22, 1943.

41. Ibid., March 3, 1944.
42. Ibid., June 6, 1944.
43. Phoenix Steel Corporation, "Company History."

Chapter 4

44. Schramm Inc., Chronology binder.
45. Schramm, "World War II Years."
46. *West Chester (PA) Daily Local News*, September 22, 1943.
47. Ibid., September 23, 1943.
48. Ibid., May 1942; June 24, 1942.
49. Schramm, "World War II Years," vol. 3.
50. Schramm Inc., Chronology binders, 1942–45.
51. *Schramm INK*, November 6, 1942.
52. Schramm, "World War II Years."
53. *Schramm INK*, October 1942.
54. Ibid., December 1943.
55. Ibid., May 7, 1943.
56. Schramm Inc. website.
57. Dixon, "Mushroom Man," 3.
58. Ibid., 1–2.
59. Rettew, *Quiet Man from West Chester*.
60. Ibid.
61. ExplorePAHistory, "Arsenal of America"; *Philadelphia Evening Bulletin*, September 3, 1943; Rettew, *Quiet Man from West Chester*, 32.
62. Rettew, *Quiet Man from West Chester*.
63. Ibid.
64. National Foam System Inc., *Keeping Pace*, 9; *West Chester (PA) Daily Local News*, "National Foam Systems Inc."
65. National Foam System Inc., *Keeping Pace*, 23–5.
66. Ibid., 24–5.
67. *West Chester (PA) Daily Local News*, June 18, 1943.
68. National Foam System Inc., *Keeping Pace*, 25.
69. The Navy "E" Award and the Army "E" Award were combined and became known as the Army-Navy "E" Award in July 1942.
70. Army-Navy Production Award Manual.
71. *West Chester (PA) Daily Local News*, December 1, 1943.
72. "From Peace to War to Peace."

73. *West Chester (PA) Daily Local News*, July 10, 1943.
74. "From Peace to War to Peace."
75. *Hist-O-Gram*, "Manufacturing Company Boomed."
76. *Hist-O-Gram*, "Downingtown MFG. Co. Played Big Role in WWII."
77. *DMC News*, May–July 1946.
78. National WWII Museum, "Rubber: A Vital WWII Commodity."
79. *DMC News*, February 1944.
80. *Hist-O-Gram*, "Manufacturing Company Boomed."
81. East Brandywine Township, "Bondsville Mill Park"; *Hist-O-Gram*, "Plaque Honors Collins & Aikman Employees Who Served in WWII."
82. Ibid.
83. East Brandywine Township, "Bondsville Mill Park"; *Hist-O-Gram*, "Plaque Honors Collins & Aikman Employees Who Served in WWII."

Chapter 5

84. Whitman, *V is for Victory*, 31.
85. Ames Historical Society, "World War II Rationing."
86. National WWII Museum, "Fun Facts about Victory Gardens."
87. "West Bradford Township Junior Fair," flyer.
88. Tredyffrin Easttown Historical Society collection, *Main Line Caller*.
89. National WWII Museum, "Rationing."
90. *Salvage*.
91. *Coatesville (PA) Record*, April 6, 1942.
92. Ibid.
93. Ibid.
94. War Production Board, *Salvage for Victory*.
95. Ibid.
96. Tredyffrin Easttown Historical Society collection, "Save Every Ounce of Waste Paper," flyer.

Chapter 6

97. Homeland Security National Preparedness Task Force, "Civil Defense and Homeland Security."
98. Encyclopedia.com, "Civil Defense."
99. *History Quarterly*, "Our Citizen Air Raid Defense Wardens."

100. Ibid., "Berwyn Lookout or Observation Point."
101. *Hist-O-Gram*, "Plane Spotting Tower."
102. *West Chester (PA) Daily Local News*, November 19, 1942.
103. "Through the War Years."
104. Chalfant, interview.
105. Mansley, "Paoli Branch," 7–9.
106. *History Quarterly*, "Our Citizen Air Raid Defense Wardens."

Chapter 7

107. *Army & Navy YMCA Bulletin*, "They Also Serve!"
108. Ibid.
109. Powell, "Fruitcake Offers Support."
110. Ibid.; YMCA, "History of the Y Logo."
111. *Coatesville Red Triangle*, December 12, 1942.
112. Ibid., January 20, 1944; February 10, 1944.
113. Ibid., July 7, 1943.
114. Ibid., July 29, 1943.
115. Ibid., May 23, 1945.
116. Ibid., Februray10, 1944; May 4, 1944.
117. YMCA of Greater Brandywine, communication with author.
118. Powell, "Fruitcake Offers Support," 2.
119. *West Chester (PA) Daily Local News*, January 4, 1946.
120. YMCA of Greater Brandywine, communication with author.

Chapter 8

121. Immaculata University, "IU History."
122. Burton, "History of Immaculata University," 42–3.
123. Ibid., 43–5.
124. Makowski, "World War II."
125. Burton, "History of Immaculata University," 46.
126. Makowski, "World War II," 18.
127. Garcia, "German POWs on the Homefront."
128. Burton, "History of Immaculata University," 46.
129. Burton, e-mail to author, August 2015.
130. Lincoln University, "About Lincoln."

131. Ibid., *Lincoln University's History of Firsts.*
132. Kraus, "CAA Helps America"; *Lincolnian*, "Aviation Finals," "'Czar' Black Gets Notice," "Flight Training in Progress at Lincoln," "Visible Effects of War Shown in Curriculum"; Harper, "World War II & The American Home Front," 22.
133. *Lincolnian*, "Air Raid Wardens and First Aiders Organized Here," 1.
134. Ibid., "Salvage Nothing New."
135. Ibid., "Defense Workers Occupy Lincoln's Oldest Dormitory," 4.
136. Ibid., "139 Lincolnmen Register for Military Service."
137. Ibid., "134 Undergraduates," 1.
138. Ibid., "Negro Personnel in Army."
139. Ibid., "NAACP Conference Huge Success," 1.
140. Ibid., "Afro Correspondent Addressed Students."
141. Lincoln University, "About Lincoln."
142. West Chester University, "History of the University."
143. West Chester State Teacher's College, "Honor Roll Book."
144. Sturzebecker, *Centennial History of West Chester*, 170.
145. West Chester University, Records of Regular Board Meeting, July 20, 1942.
146. Sturzebecker, *Centennial History of West Chester*, 170; West Chester University, 170, 172.
147. Ibid., 171; West Chester University, Records of Regular Board Meeting, March 16, 1942.
148. Ibid.
149. West Chester University, Records of Regular Board Meeting, March 16, 1942; February 15, 1943; January 6, 1944.
150. *Quad Angles*, March 10, 1944, 3; September 28, 1945, 1–2.

Chapter 9

151. National WWII Museum, "By the Numbers"; Historical Society of the Phoenixville Area, "Brief History."
152. Kathman, interview.
153. Morris, "History of the Valley Forge General Hospital."
154. Kennedy, "Former Hospital Was Haven for Wounded GIs."
155. Ibid.
156. Dixon, "Haverford History."
157. According to the Red Cross website, as the organization grew, it decided to use a color-coding system for its uniforms and pins during World War I.

The group of volunteers known as the Hostess and Hospital Service and Recreation Corps wore a gray uniform with a white collar and cuffs. The name was changed to Hospital and Recreation Corps in the 1930s, but "gray lady" was the expression commonly used. After World War II, the name of the group officially changed to the Gray Lady service.

158. *Forge*, 3.
159. Ibid., July 29, 1944, 5.
160. Ertell, "German POWS at VFGH," 2.
161. Garcia, "German POWs on the Homefront."
162. Lewis, "Nazi Captives Ready to Pull Out Copy."
163. Ertell, "German POWS at VFGH," 5.

Chapter 10

164. DHS Alumni, *Downingtown's Greatest Generation*.
165. *West Chester (PA) Daily Local News*, November 19, 1942.
166. Ibid., December 3, 1942.
167. Ibid., 1943.
168. *Oxford News*, September 13, 1945.
169. Chester County Hospital, "Chester County Hospital History."
170. "Army Airways Communication System Affidavit."
171. "Coatesville Hospital Affidavit."
172. Devlin, "In Field Near Berks Border."
173. *West Chester (PA) Daily Local News*, May 8, 1944.
174. Clark, "Milkweed Fruits: Pods of Plenty."
175. *Oxford Press*, "Farmers Urged to Aid in Milkweed Floss Harvest."
176. *West Chester (PA) Daily Local News*, August 30, 1944.
177. Ibid., June 2, 1944.
178. Ibid., September 23, 1944.
179. *Coatesville (PA) Record*, March 27, 1941.
180. Ibid., November 18, 1943.

Bibliography

Ames Historical Society. "World War II Rationing on the U.S. Homefront." http://www.ameshistory.org/exhibits/events/rationing.htm.

"Army Airways Communication System Affidavit." Reading, PA, December 6, 1943.

Army & Navy YMCA Bulletin. "They Also Serve!" November 1942.

Army-Navy Production Award Manual. Washington, D.C.: Navy and War Department.

Borough of Phoenixville. "Demographics: Phoenixville Demographics & Household Information." http://www.phoenixville.org/livinghere/21.

Burton, Sister Anne Marie, IHM. "A History of Immaculata University, 1920–2015." Malvern, PA: Immaculata University, forthcoming.

Chalfant, Margaret B. Interviewed by Marion M. Piccolomini, July 27, 2015.

Chester County. "Facts About Chester County." http://www.chesco.org/index.aspx?NID=892.

Chester County Hospital. "The Chester County Hospital History." http://www.chestercountyhospital.org/cchhist.asp?p=510.

Clark, Patterson. "Milkweed Fruits: Pods of Plenty." *Washington Post*, September 25, 2012. http://www.washingtonpost.com/wp-srv/special/metro/urban-jungle/pages/120925.html.

"Coatesville Hospital Affidavit." Letter from Major Augustus Becker. Coatesville, PA, December 7, 1943.

Coatesville (PA) Record. March 22, 1941; March 27, 1941; November 18, 1943.

———. "Parkesburg Bond Drive Is Over Top." October 2, 1943.

Coatesville Red Triangle. December 12, 1942; July 7, 1943; July 29, 1943; January 20, 1944; February 10, 1944; May 4, 1944; June 15, 1944; September 1944; May 23, 1945; March 25, 1946; May 1946.

Devlin, Ron. "In Field Near Berks Border: A World War II–Era Miracle Remembered." *Reading Eagle*, June 14, 2014. http://www.readingeagle.com/news/article/in-field-near-berks-border-a-world-war-II-era-miracle-remembered.

DHS Alumni. *Downingtown's Greatest Generation*. Cooperative project of the Downingtown Area Historical Society and the Downingtown Area High School Alumni Association. May 1, 1944.

DiOrio, Eugene L., Katherine Gould Pella and Richard P. Smith. *Remarkable Past, Promising Future: 200 Years of Iron and Steel Operations in Coatesville, PA*. Coatesville, PA: Graystone Society, 2012.

Dixon, Mark E. "Haverford History: Virginia McCall's WWII Art Advanced the Field of Plastic Surgery at Valley Forge General Hospital." *Main Line Today*, July 2013. http://www.mainlinetoday.com/Main-Line-Today/July-2013/Haverford-History-Virginia-McCalls-WWII-Art-Adv.

———. "The Mushroom Man: A Chester County Fungus Expert Helped Pioneer Production of a Drug that Saved Thousands." *Main Line Today*, March 2011. http://www.mainlinetoday.com/Main-Line-Today/March-2011/The-Mushroom-Man.

DMC News. July 1943; November 1943; February 1944; August 1944; December 1944; February 1945; December 1945; March–July 1946.

———. "Our Part in Victory." 1946.

East Brandywine Township. "Bondsville Mill Park." http://ebrandywine.org/facilities/facility/details/Bondsville-Mill-Park-13.

Encyclopedia Britannica. "Selective Training and Service Act." http://britannica.com/EBchecked/topic/533200/Selective-Training-and-Service-Act.

Encyclopedia.com. "Civil Defense." http://www.encyclopedia.com/topic/civil_defense.aspx.

Ertell, J.R. "German POWS at VFGH." Historical Society of the Phoenixville Area. September 2012. http://www.hspa-pa.org/Newsletter/2012%20Sept%20Newsletter.pdf.

ExplorePAHistory. "The Arsenal of America: Pennsylvania During the Second War." http://explorepahistory.com/story.php?storyId=1-9-19&chapter=3.

———. "G. Raymond Rettew Historical Marker." http://explorepahistory.com/hmarker.php?markerId=1-A-2F2.

———. "G. Raymond Rettew on the Production of Penecillin During World War II." http://explorepahistory.com/odocument.php?docId=1-4-18C.

———. "Stories from PA History: The Vision of William Penn." http://explorepahistory.com/story.php?storyId=1-9-3.

Forge, the. December 30, 1944.

———. "Malvern Man Donates $500 Phone Fund." July 29, 1944.

———. "Paratroopers Describe D-Day in Normandy." July 29, 1944.

Freeman, Larry. "Liberty Ship S.S. *John W. Brown* Lecture," National Steel & Iron Heritage Museum. May 2014. http://www.steelmuseum.org/video/2014/john_brown_lecture_5_1_14.cfm.

"From Peace to War to Peace." West Chester, PA: National Foam Systems Inc.

Garcia, J. Malcolm. "German POWs on the Homefront." September 15, 2009. Smithsonian.com. http://www.smithsonianmag.com/history/german-pows-on-the-american-homefront-141009996/?no-ist.

Groff, Virginia C. Interviewed by Marion M. Piccolomini, May 27, 2015; November 12, 2015.

Harper, Marilyn. "World War II & The American Home Front: A National Historic Landmarks Theme Study." October 2007. http://www.nps.gov/nhl/learn/themes/WWIIHomeFront.pdf.

Harris, Mary U., ed. *Significant Events in the United States Civil Defense History.* Washington, D.C.: Defense Civil Preparedness Agency, 1975. http://www.civildefensemuseum.com/history.html.

Hist-O-Gram. "Downingtown MFG. Co. Played Big Role in WWII." August 2, 2012. http://www.downingtownareahistoricalsociety.org/Histograms/2012%20Hist-O-Grams/Aug%20-Oct%202012.pdf.

———. "Manufacturing Company Boomed for Many Years." August 2, 2012. http://www.downingtownareahistoricalsociety.org/Histograms/2012%20Hist-O-Grams/Aug%20-Oct%202012.pdf.

———. "Plane Spotting Tower Was Located at McIlvaine Farm." May 9, 2013. http://www.downingtownareahistoricalsociety.org/Histograms/2013%20Hist-O-Grams/May%209%202013%20Hist-O-Gram.pdf.

———. "Plaque Honors Collins & Aikman Employees Who Served in WWII." May 9, 2013. http://www.downingtownareahistoricalsociety.org/Histograms/2013%20Hist-O-Grams/May%209%202013%20Hist-O-Gram.pdf.

Historical Society of the Phoenixville Area. "A Brief History of Valley Forge General Hospital." http://www.hspa-pa.org/History%20of%20Valley%20Forge%20Army%20Hospital.pdf.

History.com. "American Women in World War II." http://www.history.com/topics/world-war-ii/american-women-in-world-war-ii.

History Place. "Franklin D. Roosevelt for a Declaration of War." http://www.historyplace.com/speeches/fdr-infamy.htm.

History Quarterly. "The Berwyn Lookout or Observation Point." Vol. 5, no. 1 (1942). http://tehistory.org/hqdav/html/v05/v05n1p004.html.

———. "Our Citizen Air Raid Defense Wardens." Vol. 5, no. 1 (1942). http://www.tehistory.org/hqda/html/v05/v05n1p005.html.

———. "Summary of the Activities of the Paoli Branch, American Red Cross." Vol. 5, no. 3 (1943). http://www.tehistory.org/hqda/html/v05/v05n3p070.html.

Homeland Security National Preparedness Task Force. "Civil Defense and Homeland Security: A Short History of National Preparedness Efforts." September 2006. https://training.fema.gov/hiedu/docs/dhs%20civil%20defense-hs%20-%20short%20history.pdf.

Honey Brook (PA) Herald. November 18, 1945; September 27, 1945.

Immaculata University. "IU History." http://www.immaculata.edu/about-iu/history.

Kathman, John. Interviewed by Marion M. Piccolomini, May 15, 2015.

Kennedy, Joseph S. "Former Hospital Was Haven for Wounded GIs Valley Forge General Hospital Specialized in Plastic Surgery, the Blind and Psychiatry." January 26, 1997. http://articles.philly.com/1997-01-26/news/25561193_1_plastic-surgery-ca.

Klein, Maury. *A Call to Arms: Mobilizing America for World War II*. New York: Bloomsbury Press, 2013.

Kraus, Theresa L. "The CAA Helps America Prepare for World War II." https://www.faa.gov/about/history/milestones/media/The_CAA_Helps_America_Prepare_for_World_WarII.pdf.

Lewis, Thomas E. "Nazi Captives Ready to Pull Out Copy of Geneva Rules at Drop of a Hat." *Philadelphia Evening Bulletin*, 1945.

Lincolnian. June 1942; December 14, 1943.

———. "Afro Correspondent Addressed Students." June 2, 1944.

———. "Air Raid Wardens and First Aiders Organized Here." March 24, 1942.

———. "Aviation Finals." January 29, 1941.

———. "'Czar' Black Gets Notice." March 6, 1943.

———. "Defense Workers Occupy Lincoln's Oldest Dormitory." October 29, 1943.

———. "Flight Training in Progress at Lincoln." October 1940.

———. "NAACP Conference Huge Success: Delegates Hear Eleanor Roosevelt Expresses Hope for Post-War World." December 14, 1943.

———. "Negro Personnel in Army Totals over 450,000." April 20, 1943.

———. "134 Undergraduates Now in Armed Forces." December 14, 1943.

———. "139 Lincolnmen Register for Military Service Under U.S. Selective Service Act: Oxford Officials Conduct Student Registration." October 19, 1940.

———. "Salvage Nothing New." December 1942.

———. "Visible Effects of War Shown in Curriculum." March 24, 1942.

Lincoln University. "About Lincoln: A Legacy of Producing Leaders." http://www.lincoln.edu/about.html.

———. *Lincoln University's History of Firsts & Other Distinctions.* Lincoln, PA: Lincoln University. http://www.lincoln.edu/PDF/Lincoln-History-of-Firsts-from-SM12-19-14.pdf.

Lindsey, John. *World War II in Numbers: An Infographic Guide to the Conflict, Its Conduct, and Its Casualties.* London: Firefly Books Ltd., 2013.

Lukens Plate, December 26, 1941; February 6, 1942; April 3, 1942; September 4, 1942; October 30, 1942; February 5, 1943; January 21, 1944; August 31, 1945.

———. "Greeting Lady." October 30, 1942.

———. "New Service Flag." January 1944.

Makowski, Toni Iaquinto. "World War II: The Immaculata Story." *Immaculata Today* (Fall): 18–9.

Mansley, Ruth D.L. "The Paoli Branch of the American Red Cross." Tredyffrin Easttown Historical Society, History Quarterly Digital Archives. 1942. http://www.tehistory.org/hqda/html/v05/v05n1p007.html.

Marryat, J.B. "Penicillin Produced Night and Day at West Chester Mushroom Plant." *Philadelphia Evening Bulletin*, September 3, 1943.

Martinez, Julia C. "Paying Honor to a Woman of Steel Long Before the Women's Movement, Rebecca Lukens Broke Barriers." Philly.com. January 6, 1994. http://articles.philly.com/1994-01-06/business/25822150_1_steel-quaker-mill.

Phoenixville (PA) Daily Republician. October 19, 1940; May 21, 1941; June 2, 1941; May 25, 1942; January 11, 1943; September 22, 1943; March 3, 1944; June 6, 1944; July 1949.

———. "CIO Votes to End Iron Co. Strike: Organizer Leaves." June 2, 1941.

———. "Phoenix Iron Company Strike Continues: SWOC Ignore NLRB Ruling." May 19, 1941.

———. "Phoenix Iron Plant Shut Down as Result of Strike, Company Forced to Abandon Operations: Selling Materials." May 21, 1941.

———. "Roosevelt—And Iron Company Strike, an Editorial." May 28, 1941.

Morris, Galloway. "A History of the Valley Forge General Hospital." *Schuykill Township News* (Spring 1998).

National Foam System Inc. *Keeping Pace, 1819–1976*. N.p., 1976.

National Iron & Steel Heritage Museum archives, Coatesville, PA, 2015.

National Park Service. "Airmen Overview." http://www.nps.gov/museum/exhibits/tuskegee/airoverview.htm.

National WWII Museum. "By the Numbers: The US Military." http://www.nationalww2museum.org/learn/education/for-students/ww2-history/ww2-by-the-numbers/us-military.html.

———. "Fun Facts about Victory Gardens." http://www.nationalww2museum.org/learn/education/for-students/ww2-history/at-a-glance/victory-gardens.html.

———. "Rationing." http://www.nww2m.com/tag/rationing.

———. "Rubber: A Vital WWII Commodity," http://www.nationalww2museum.org/assets/pdfs/rubber-in-world-war-ii-fact.pdf.

———. "Take a Closer Look at the Draft." http://www.nationalww2museum.org/learn/education/for-students/ww2-history/take-a-closer-look/draft-registration-documents.html?referrer=https://www.google.com.

———. "Timeline." http://www.nationalww2museum.org/history/final/interactive_timeline.html.

———. "WWII Veterans Statistics." http://www.nationalww2museum.org/honor/wwii-veterans-statistics.html.

Oxford News. September 13, 1945.

Oxford Press. November 1942.

———. "Farmers Urged to Aid in Milkweed Floss Harvest." August 30, 1944.

Philadelphia Evening Bulletin. September 3, 1943.

Philadelphia Inquirer. "Phoenix Iron & Steel Company has Changed Its Name to Phoenix Steel Corporation." January 26, 1959.

Phoenix Steel Corporation. "Company History." Phoenixville, PA: Historical Society of Phoenixville Area.

Powell, Pam. "Fruitcake Offers Support to Troops During Wartime." *West Chester (PA) Daily Local News*. http://www.dailylocal.com/article/DL/20071214/TMP01/312149984.

Quad Angles. March 10, 1944.

———. "Changes in *Quad Angles* Necessitated by War." September 24, 1943: 2.

———. "Peace Brings Changes to West Chester Campus." September 28, 1945.

———. "West Chester Without War." September 28, 1945.

Rettew, G. Raymond. *A Quiet Man from West Chester*. West Chester, PA: Chester County Historical Society, 1974.

Roosevelt, Franklin D. "104—Address at Shibe Park." American Presidency Project. Philadelphia, PA, October 27, 1944. http://www.presidency.ucsb.edu/ws/?pid=16458.

Salvage. Pamphlet. Hagley Museum and Library.

Schramm, Harold J. "The World War II Years." In Chronology binder. Vol. 2. West Chester, PA, 1940–46.

Schramm Inc. Chronology binders. Vols. 1–3. West Chester, PA, 1940–46.

———. http://www.schramminc.com.

Schramm INK. October 1942; November 6, 1942; May 7, 1943; December 1943; July 1944; August 1945; December 1945.

———. "Sports Chatter." October 1944.

———. "To the Ladies." November 6, 1942.

Sheehan, Sean. *The Technology of World War II*. New York: Raintree Steck-Vaughn Publishers, 2003.

Sturzebecker, Russell L. *The Centennial History of West Chester State College*. West Chester, PA, 1996. http://www.wcupa.edu/library.fhg/special_collections/exhibits/centennial_history/Introduction/toc.html.

"Through the War Years with Southeastern Pennsylvania Chapter—American Red Cross." December 2, 1946.

Tredyffrin Easttown Historical Society collection. *Main Line Caller*.

———. "Save Every Ounce of Waste Paper," Flyer.

United States Bureau of the Census. *No. 1430, Employment Status of the Civilian Population: 1929–1998*. Washington, D.C.: United States Government Printing Office, 1999.

———. *Sixteenth Census of the United States: 1940: Population*. Vol. 1. Washington, D.C.: United States Government Printing Office, 1942.

War Production Board. Bureau of Industrial Conservation. *Salvage for Victory*. Washington, D.C.: War Production Board.

"West Bradford Township Junior Fair" Flyer. Chester County Historical Society.

West Chester (PA) Daily Local News, January 18, 1942; May 1942; June 24, 1942; November 19, 1942; December 3, 1942; June 16, 1943; June 18, 1943; July 10, 1943; September 22, 1943; September 23, 1943; November 2, 1943; December 1, 1943; September 4, 1944; May 8, 1944; June 2, 1944; August 30, 1944; September 23, 1944.

———. "Hitler Pushes Way into Poland; 310 Americans Are Saved as Ship Sinks." September 3, 1939.

———. "National Foam System Inc. Leads the Nation in the Science of Fire-Fighting." January 28, 1957.

———. "YMCA Mails 'Triangles' at Coatesville." January 4, 1946.

West Chester State Teacher's College. "Honor Roll Book." West Chester, PA: State Teacher's College, May 1945.

West Chester University. "History of the University." https://www.wcupa.edu/_services/stu.nsp/parentHandbook/history.aspx.

———. Records of Regular Board Meeting. July 20, 1921; March 16, 1942; February 15, 1943; January 6, 1944.

Whiteman, LeRoy. Interviewed by Marion M. Piccolomini. September 2, 2015.

Whitman, Sylvia. *V is for Victory*. Minneapolis, MN: Lerner Publishing, 1993.

YMCA. E-mail with the author.

———. "The History of the Y Logo." http://www.ymca.net/sites/default/files/pdf/y-logo-history.pdf.

———. "The Story of Our Founding." http://www.ymca.net/history/founding.html.

———. "YMCA of Brandywine Valley 2014 Annual Report." 2014.

Index

E

F

G

H

I

J

L

M

N

O

P

Q

R

S

T

U

V

W

Y

About the Author

Marion is the daughter of a World War II veteran. She is an officer of the Downingtown Area Historical Society and is a member of the West Nantmeal Township Historical Commission. She holds a master's degree in speech language pathology from the Pennsylvania State University, having worked in the medical industry, college and private practice fields. She currently resides in Chester County with her family.

Visit us at
www.historypress.net

This title is also available as an e-book